JOHN DON'''

Literary Lives
General Editor: Richard Dutton, Professor of English
Lancaster University

This series offers stimulating accounts of the literary careers of
the most admired and influential English-language authors.
Volumes follow the outline of the writers' working lives, not
in the spirit of traditional biography, but aiming to trace
the professional, publishing and social contexts which
shaped their writing.

A list of the published titles in the series follows overleaf.

Published titles

Cedric C. Brown
JOHN MILTON

Peter Davison
GEORGE ORWELL

Richard Dutton
WILLIAM SHAKESPEARE

Jan Fergus
JANE AUSTEN

James Gibson
THOMAS HARDY

Kenneth Graham
HENRY JAMES

Paul Hammond
JOHN DRYDEN

W. David Kay
BEN JONSON

Mary Lago
E. M. FORSTER

Clinton Machann
MATTHEW ARNOLD

Alasdair D. F. Macrae
W. B. YEATS

Joseph McMinn
JONATHAN SWIFT

Kerry McSweeney
GEORGE ELIOT

John Mepham
VIRGINIA WOOLF

Michael O'Neill
PERCY BYSSHE SHELLEY

Leonée Ormond
ALFRED TENNYSON

Harold Pagliaro
HENRY FIELDING

George Parfitt
JOHN DONNE

Gerald Roberts
GERARD MANLEY HOPKINS

Felicity Rosslyn
ALEXANDER POPE

Tony Sharpe
T. S. ELIOT

Grahame Smith
CHARLES DICKENS

Gary Waller
EDMUND SPENSER

Cedric Watts
JOSEPH CONRAD

John Williams
WILLIAM WORDSWORTH

Tom Winnifrith and Edward Chitham
CHARLOTTE AND EMILY BRONTË

John Worthen
D. H. LAWRENCE

John Donne

A Literary Life

George Parfitt

Reader in English Literature
University of Nottingham

MACMILLAN

First published 1989 by
MACMILLAN PRESS LTD
Houndmills, Basingstoke, Hampshire RG21 6XS
and London
Companies and representatives
throughout the world

ISBN 0–333–42212–0 hardcover
ISBN 0–333–42213–9 paperback

A catalogue record for this book is available
from the British Library.

This book is printed on paper suitable for recycling and
made from fully managed and sustained forest sources.

10   9   8   7   6   5   4   3   2
07   06   05   04   03   02   01   00   99

Printed in Great Britain by
Antony Rowe Ltd, Chippenham, Wiltshire

For Jessica

Contents

Preface   viii

1 1572–1601   1

   I   Biographical Outline   1
   II Aspiration   3
   III The Pattern Revolved   7
   IV Satire and Environment   13
   V Poems and Women (i)   30

2 1601–1615   40

   I   Biographical Outline   40
   II Aspiration and Frustration   44
   III Towards Ordination   54
   IV Writings: Survey and Milieu   63
   V Poems and Woman (ii)   72
   VI Poems and God   88

3 1613–1632   101

   I   Biographical Outline   101
   II Donne and Preaching   104
   III Doctrine   110
   IV Sermons as Product   115
   V Depression and Death   121

An Appendix on Criticism of Donne's Writing   126

Notes   129

Bibliography   137

Index   139

Preface

This is a short book and does not set out to deal even-handedly with all aspects of Donne's life and work. It tries instead to concentrate on examining selected aspects of this life and work in the context of the times Donne lived in, and it seeks to emphasise those features which are most alive in our times. This means, in particular, emphasis upon the period between Donne's marriage in 1601 and his ordination in 1615. The last period of his life and its main literary product, the sermons, are treated more briefly because they have limited interest now, for reasons which are sketched in Chapter 3, while the treatment of the early years is limited by the gaps in the surviving evidence.

I have made direct use of very little literary criticism of Donne's work. This is mainly because, as suggested in the bibliographical essay in the Appendix, much of what has been written is either too heavily of the school of New Criticism to be of much use here, or is concerned with literary tradition rather than with the type of context which this series treats of. It should, however, be added that my understanding of Donne's work has certainly been much influenced over the years by earlier criticism.

I should like to thank the General Editor of the series, Dr Richard Dutton, for asking me to write this volume and for his help throughout its gestation. Also, my thanks, as always, to my wife, Maureen Bell, for her patience and understanding at a time when she has been busy with her own research and when our small daughter has kept us both occupied.

George Parfitt

1

1572–1601

There is a standard biography of John Donne, the author of which, R. C. Bald, has drawn together what is known of Donne's life and has supplemented the facts with his knowledge of the relevant period, while remaining properly aware of what we do not know.[1] John Carey has written what might be called a 'spiritual biography', an account of 'the distinctive structure of Donne's imagination'[2] which uses cross-references between works and life as well as between one work and another to define that imagination. Other writers have, like Alan Sinfield,[3] put less weight upon Donne's individualism and more upon how he relates to culture and society in his period. Here Carey's romanticism and liberalism give way to a more materialistic stress.

A book as short as the present one cannot hope to match Bald's fullness; nor can it present the sort of critique needed to expose Carey's serious limitations and to show how a materialistic enquiry can avoid reductivism.[4] It can, however, hope to be lucid while indicating something of Donne's complexity and significance.

I BIOGRAPHICAL OUTLINE

John Donne married Ann More in December 1601, when he was around thirty years old and she was about sixteen. Although popular belief is that our ancestors married young it was in fact common for marriage to be delayed until the male was financially in a position to support a wife. Moreover, despite Juliet, Ann More was young for an Elizabethan or Jacobean bride.[5] Donne's marriage, as is widely known, was one of the decisive events of his life, a life which, as we might expect, is lightly documented up to this time. Bald's account of the first thirty years of Donne's life occupies less than a quarter of his book, and much of this space is devoted to the poet's ancestry and environment. An outline of Donne's life up to 1601 can, therefore, be presented quite tersely.

He was born in 1572. His father was a successful London ironmonger who had been made a freeman of the Ironmongers' Company, 'probably before the end of 1556'[6] and who had married Elizabeth Heywood around 1564. When Donne's father died early in 1576, six children survived him and some six months after her first husband's death Elizabeth remarried, the spouse being John Syminges, a doctor who was several times President of the Royal College of Physicians. It is perhaps worth remarking that this re-marriage did not involve a decisive social move upwards, as might at first appear. Donne's father was a substantial business-man whose master, Thomas Lewen, had been a Sheriff of London in 1537/8 and who left a considerable estate at his death, while physicians in the sixteenth century were not of great social standing.[7]

It is not surprising that the first decade of Donne's life is largely blank now. Elizabethan record-keeping was primitive by our standards; John Donne was only one of several children; and Elizabethan children were not usually considered interesting in themselves.[8] We might, however, expect some references to his schooling, if not from surviving records at least in later statements by the poet himself or by contemporaries. But no such statements survive and Izaak Walton tells us that Donne 'had his first breeding in his Fathers house, where a private Tutor had the care of him, until the tenth year of his age'.[9]

What we call tertiary education began and ended sooner in the sixteenth century than it does now, and in October 1584 John Donne, with his brother Henry, went to Hart Hall, Oxford, where he remained for about three years. This takes us to late 1587, but then another blank occurs. We know that the poet entered Thavies Inn in 1591 before going on to Lincoln's Inn in May 1592, where he was based until at least late 1594. What, then, was Donne doing between late 1587 and 1591? Walton claims that, 'About the fourteenth year of his age [Donne] was translated from Oxford to Cambridge; where . . . he staied till his seventeenth year',[10] and if this is true the gap is substantially accounted for. In itself, what Walton claims is plausible enough, although Donne's name does not appear in the defective Cambridge records.[11] But Walton also speaks of Donne staying 'some years in Italy, and then in Spain' and locates these years after 1597.[12] This, however, is scarcely possible (as we shall see) and it has been suggested that this period of travel on the continent may have been between 1587 and 1591, either to the exclusion of Cambridge or as well as time there.[13] It seems unlikely that Walton is completely wrong about the travelling, but, writing well after 1600,[14] he may have been imprecise both about the sequence of events and the duration of the journey ('some years').

We know that Donne was a volunteer on the Essex expeditions to Cadiz in 1596 and to the Azores in the following year. We also know that he came to the attention of Sir Thomas Egerton, Lord Keeper of the Great Seal, presumably through acquaintance with the younger Thomas Egerton, and that he was one of Egerton's secretaries from November 1597 or early 1598 until his marriage in 1601. This makes it unlikely that he travelled, as Walton claims, in these years. Just before marriage, Donne became an MP for Brackley in Northamptonshire (the seat being controlled by Egerton) and was given a grant by the crown of some land in Lincolnshire, this entitling him, as Carey points out, to call himself 'esquire'.[15]

This is only an outline. It takes the few hard facts we have and arranges them in order as best we can, the facts not always being chronologically very firmly fixed and their ordering sometimes suspect. At all points the outline could be filled in with plausible inferences designed to amplify our understanding of Donne's first thirty years (which was itself a full lifetime by Elizabethan standards)[16] by linking this outline with what we know of late-Elizabethan social, cultural and political history. But it may be more useful to concentrate only upon selected aspects of an early life which is, or appears to be, a familiar Elizabethan pattern. This is the concern of the next section.

II ASPIRATION

Donne's father, we have noted, was a successful ironmonger in London and this places him firmly in the merchant class. But we need to notice two things at once. The first is that no such class is recognised in Elizabethan theory. Obviously trade exists, but it does not fit in with the accepted social hierarchy, having only a shadowy existence somewhere between 'gentry' and 'peasant'.[17] The second point is that this imprecision of category is both significant and revealing. On the one hand, there is plenty of

evidence of self-consciousness among merchants,[18] while the fact
that the category of merchant has only a shadowy formal existence
arises partly because the category itself is a very flexible one. This
flexibility in turn reflects the social mobility which existed in
Elizabethan reality, even while society was officially severely
compartmentalised. It was not uncommon for the younger sons
of gentry to go into trade, or for sons of tradespeople to follow a
social pattern which established them as genteel (or even, as with
Lionel Cranfield, led to ennoblement).[19] Social aspiration was
common and this is the key to John Donne's first thirty years. It
can be studied both in relation to his ancestry and in the context
of his education and employment.

Put rather crudely, what is involved is the suppression of one
category (trade) in favour of another (gentry). Donne himself
never draws attention to his mercantile background nor
emphasises the genteel element in his ancestry. But Izaak Walton
works the available material over most artfully. First of all he
suggests that Donne's ancestry is unimportant, for 'his own
Learning and other multiplyed merits may justly appear sufficient
to dignifie both Himself and his Posterity'.[20] For anyone who will
judge fairly, Walton suggests, learning and merit will entitle
Donne to dignity (social standing) and also dignify his posterity.
In other words, Donne's learning and merit will make him genteel
and gentrify his family.

Walton, then, nevertheless tells his readers that Donne's 'Father
was masculinely and lineally descended from a very antient
Family in Wales, where many of his name now live, that deserve
and have great reputation in that Countrey'[21] – and here the key
words are 'lineally', 'antient' and 'reputation', providing a patina
of gentility, with no mention of trade. But there is more detail
when Walton turns to the maternal line: 'By his Mother he was
descended of the Family of the famous and learned Sir Thomas
Moor, sometime Lord Chancellour of England: as also, from that
worthy and laborious Judge Rastall, who left Posterity the vast
Statutes of the Law of this Nation most exactly abridged'.[22]

In these opening two paragraphs of his 'Life', Walton has
selected to good effect. Donne does not, it is suggested, need an
ancestry, but he is nonetheless given one, and the nature of
Walton's account reminds us of the Elizabethan and Jacobean
passion for proving genteel and noble ancestry, a passion which
is more than mere snobbery.[23] It is proper, in terms of hierarchy,

that paternal ancestry is dealt with first,[24] but Walton is vague about the dignifying Welsh connexion and chooses to ignore the London trade element which he could presumably have filled in with little trouble had he wished. When he turns to the maternal line he can offer dignifying names – More and Rastall – but he silently ignores the martyrdom of Thomas More and also disguises the literary element in Donne's background. More is not here a writer, while Rastall is an abridger of legal statutes rather than the author of *The Four Elements* and Walton makes no reference to the fact that Donne's mother was the youngest daughter of John Heywood, epigrammatist and writer of interludes.

What Walton is doing is to make over Donne's ancestry in terms suitable to the dignitary of the Anglican faith which, in the last years of his life, Donne actually became. This Walton version is not dishonest, or even factually inaccurate, but it repeats a transformation which Donne himself sought to make, first in one context, then in another.

This becomes clear if we look again at our outline: university, foreign travel, Inns of Court, military service, secretary to Egerton. There is a common objective or focus for all this, the Court. Put another way, the pattern is one designed to maximise opportunities for a career in and around Court, and the latter has to be seen as the true centre of the Elizabethan social and political world. The great offices of state are still truly Crown offices, appointments in the monarch's gift rather than made by a Prime Minister; the Privy Council is the monarch's cabinet, to debate, advise and implement policy as and when the Crown dictates. Court is also the place of social preferment. If one caught the monarch's eye everything might follow (as it did for Elizabeth's Leicester and James' Buckingham) and follow very quickly (although it should be noted that everything could also fall away as quickly), while the importance of favourites means that opportunities also arose for careers in serving favourites.[25] Attention to serving a favourite or great officer of state is a way of creating possibilities of becoming a favourite or officer oneself, Francis Bacon being only the most famous example.[26]

By 1584 a period at university was less a route into the church than it had been (although it could still be that) and for many it led into what we might loosely and anachronistically call the civil service. Attendance at a university was not necessary as part of the training of a gentleman (and still less so for a son of the nobility) but it could be useful, and was certainly so for the aspirant to gentility.[27] Equally, while many of the gentry did not go to the Inns of Court many did[28] and this was another posting-stage on the road to gentility for some non-genteel males. While knowledge of the law would help young men with lands to inherit in a litigious society, it is more important to note that the location of the Inns provided opportunities for young men to draw the attention of the Court proper. As for travel abroad it can be seen as significant in two ways, both of them relevant to a Court career. In so far as it gave the traveller some knowledge of foreign societies and cultures it can be seen as helping to make the complete courtier.[29] This can be given a more practical gloss. In the absence of modern communications, foreign affairs obvious-ly depended heavily upon diplomacy, but Elizabethan diplomacy remained extremely amateur. There were few permanent postings and few career diplomats. Postings abroad and diplomatic missions were valuable ways of gaining and maintaining the monarch's favour, although it is also true that being sent abroad could be a sign of disfavour, almost of exile, and taking on a major diplomatic or military mission abroad might be to gamble with your courtly power-base.[30] Gaining some knowledge of foreign countries as a young man could obviously help such a man to work his way into office and favour. Finally, when military expeditions occurred, joining them was a clear way of demonstrating spirit and willingness to serve Queen and country.[31]

When John Donne became one of Sir Thomas Egerton's secretar-ies he had successfully completed the apprenticeship of a gentle-man, and the grant of land mentioned earlier can be seen as certification that this son of a London ironmonger was now of the gentry. Moreover, to be secretary to the Lord Keeper was to be well placed to rise higher in the service of the Crown.

There is, I think, no evidence that Donne ever expected, was expected, or was inclined to follow either his father's trade or his first step-father's profession; unlike Ben Jonson who was, for a time, a bricklayer like his step-father. There is also no hint that he might have thought of carrying forward the maternal links with the stage seen in Rastall and John Heywood. What there is, it seems, is a typical pattern, its purpose being to make a gentleman, specifically a gentleman about the Court.

III THE PATTERN REVOLVED

But if we look again at the pattern of Donne's first thirty years we may begin to see that it does not fit exactly into that of aspirant to the gentry. There is one main reason for this: Catholicism.

It was mentioned earlier that Walton ignores the martyrdom of Thomas More. There is no way in which the sympathetic biographer of the late dean of St Paul's would wish to draw attention to More's refusal to accept the Henrican break with Rome, a refusal sustained to the point of execution. But Walton's suppressions go further than this. Donne's maternal grandfather, John Heywood, fled with his wife to Louvain in 1564 rather than conform; another Heywood, Thomas, was executed in 1574 for saying mass. Two of John Heywood's sons, Ellis and Jasper, became Jesuits; Donne's mother (as Walton does record later in his account) 'remained a devout Catholic until her death'; Donne's brother Henry died in Newgate in 1593, having been arrested for harbouring a Catholic priest in his chambers at Lincoln's Inn. Donne's father also seems to have been a Romanist, and there are other possible Catholic links.[32]

The fact that John Donne was born into a Catholic family probably explains why he seems not to have gone to school and is almost certainly the reason why he went up to Oxford so young. Since the 1581 Oxford Statute of Matriculation required students over sixteen to accept both the Act of Supremacy and the Thirty-Nine Articles[33] it is obvious that the earlier Donne started at Oxford the longer he could stay. But since the Act required all candidates for degrees to acknowledge the royal supremacy Donne could not officially graduate while remaining a Catholic.[34]

The situation of Catholics in England during the last decades of the sixteenth century is not easy to generalise about accurately. Even before 1570 they were formally heavily disadvantaged, their loyalty to the state in doubt, their lives and property open to attacks,[35] although it seems that no Catholic lay-person was executed between 1558 and 1570 and token conformity, or simply a low profile, could mean a relatively untroubled life for many. It is also clear that many looked for quiet survival rather than a martyr's crown in the early years of Elizabeth's reign. This may have been so partly because the future must have seemed unclear to many. It would not have been absurd to envisage that England might again become a Catholic state by monarchic decision.[36] The movement to quite extreme Protestantism under Edward VI had, after all, been followed by reversion to Catholicism under Mary. Elizabeth's religious preferences were hard to discern and a Catholic successor was far from impossible, even if Elizabeth herself did not marry a Catholic prince. But between 1570 and 1600 several events put English Catholics under greater pressure.

In 1570 itself the Papal Bull which excommunicated Elizabeth was promulgated. If Elizabeth was, as the Bull claimed, a heretic it could follow that the duty of Catholics was to reject her sovereignty and to seek to wipe it out, even by assassination. Within English Catholicism there were fears that the Bull would imperil native Catholics and serious doubts about the validity of the Bull's decrees. But the Bull was a propaganda gift to the Elizabethan government in so far as it made it easy to present Catholics as subversive. Although Catholics could and did argue that they could be loyal to the state while continuing to be Catholics,[37] this view sat uneasily beside the claims of the Papal Bull and was contrary to the strongly held belief that religious uniformity was necessary for state security.

Two years before the Bull was promulgated two significant things had happened: the Douai seminary was set up to train priests to work in England for the re-conversion of that country to Catholicism; and Mary of Scots took refuge in England. Mary had a very strong claim to the succession to the English throne and she was a Catholic. Her existence was a threat to English Protestantism and particularly so while she was physically present in the country. Even if the Catholic plots associated with her were in fact largely engineered by the English government, as Southwell argues, they stand as symbols of that threat and of Mary herself as a focus for Protestant fears. As for the seminary at Douai, it represents a move among some Catholics from passivity to activity and a recognition that re-conversion was unlikely to occur without some prompting. Given the association between uniformity and security mentioned above, however, Catholic claims that Douai (and later Jesuit) missionaries were operating only at a spiritual level were hardly likely to be accepted by the English government, while anti-Catholic legislation made such missionaries necessarily clandestine figures.

The first Douai priests reached England in 1574, two years after the St Bartholomew's Day massacre in France had undercut beliefs that Catholic and Protestant might be able to co-exist peacefully in one state. The number of priests arriving was never very large (36 in 1583 seems to be the largest figure in any one year of the century) but some 200 Catholics were executed between 1570 and 1603, mainly for treason. Executions were meant to deter and were as vile as one can imagine. The pressing of Mary Clitheroe and the torture and execution of Edmund Campion reflect little credit on anyone except the victims, but such events do illustrate both the fortitude of the committed Catholic minority and the fears the government had about the Catholic threat, fears which were exacerbated by the Armada crisis of 1588 and by other rumoured and actual preparations for invasion by the Spanish. Such events, of course, seemed to give the lie to the claim that English Catholics could be loyal to the state, even though the behaviour of English Catholics during the Armada crisis gave substance to that claim.[38]

At one extreme, then, there is the grim reality of the executions, of priests and lay-people mangled for their faith (the Catholic viewpoint) or for subversion (the state's account). Given the anti-Catholic legislation which existed, and the more hard-line readings of what faith in the Church of Rome required, execution was a theoretical possibility for any English Catholic so long as he or she remained faithful. Exactly how real this threat was cannot be demonstrated with any precision. We cannot even say much that is statistically revealing, since the 200 Catholic executions cannot be precisely related to the Catholic population, which is unknowable now. Various degrees of evasion, protection and partial conformity were possible, while geographical distance from London may have increased security. Most Catholics may have lived out their lives without at any time coming close to serious danger. Yet two points can be made. One is that both government and Catholic propagandists had good reason to give wide and vivid publicity to the executions. For the government this could serve both to warn all Catholics of the dangers inherent in their position and all citizens of the perils of deviation from utter loyalty to the state and its church. Catholics could use the same propaganda to demonstrate the brutality of the state, thus appealing to Catholic solidarity and to pride in the sacrifice made by co-religionists. In a sense, therefore, the number of executions is less important than the publicity given to them. Secondly, the chances of prison, torture and execution obviously increased considerably when a Catholic adopted an active role. The priests themselves are examples of this, but their presence in England depended upon other Catholics harbouring them and helping them in various ways. Hearing mass was dangerous and the training of priests to make it possible for English Catholics to be spiritually serviced made the position of such Catholics within English society more precarious.

Donne was born into a Catholic family and the record of his first thirty years is, as we have seen, one of aspiration to the condition of English gentleman. Even if no such aspiration had existed Donne's situation would not have been easy. As a Catholic he would have been vulnerable in the way discussed above, but as a Catholic with a family background of prominent Catholicism his position would have been the more exposed, with Jesuits among his relatives and executions on the record. This, though, can be seen either negatively, as the danger of imprisonment and execution, or positively, as the possibility of the religious glory of martyrdom.

We have little evidence of Donne's spiritual life before 1601. As we shall see, the early writings suggest that the spiritual was less important to him than the social, but this evidence may be misleading, and if we back-project the strenuous nature of Donne's finest religious writing upon the early decades of his life it can be suggested that those decades were less firmly secular than some of the early poems and the famous character sketch by Richard Baker suggest.[39] But whatever inner struggles may have been going on, the outer pattern of these decades is of social aspiration, and here Donne's Catholicism could only be a disadvantage.

A Catholic could not officially graduate (not necessarily a serious disadvantage) and he could not expect to hold office in the state, to be accepted to service in Court or with its great men. There are exceptions, but the point is that success as a Catholic in the Elizabethan state depended upon making some accommodation between religious faith and secular ambition – and, short of evident, even zealous, conformity, a person of Catholic family remained vulnerable. John Donne could hardly have been unaffected, for example, by the arrest of his priest-harbouring brother in 1593.

This takes us into difficult territory: what do we understand by Donne's career up to 1601, in the context of Catholicism? Negatives may help here. Ellis and Jasper Heywood became Jesuits, but Donne did not go to Douai, Rheims or Rome. He made no moves that we know of to prepare for an active Catholic role. But up to the time he left Lincoln's Inn he had done nothing inconsistent with fidelity to his faith. Bald tells us that Hart Hall 'had the reputation of being a centre for Catholics'[40] and the fact that it had no chapel would have made life easier for Catholics there. Catholics also frequented the Inns of Court.[41] After all, despite government doubts, Catholics might be of English blood, and might be genteel or genteel aspirant. As we shall see, the facts that Donne was writing verse at Lincoln's Inn and seems to have been involved with revels there suggest an active bid to be noticed by the Elizabethan Court, which is not strictly compatible with firm Catholicism, but this is hardly conclusive evidence that he had reached some position of compromise, for Donne could have been trying to exemplify Catholic loyalty to the state rather than conformity to the state religion.

When Donne joined the Essex expeditions of 1596 and 1597 he actively signalled his claims to gentility and his commitment to the service of the state. By serving against the great Catholic enemy, Spain, he exemplifies Catholic willingness to 'render unto Caesar . . .', or, to put this more teasingly, the ability to make some separation between the spiritual and the temporal. Robert Southwell would have approved. How Catholic Donne was by 1596, or how far he had moved away from Catholicism, we simply do not know. All that can be said is that a hard-line Catholic could scarcely have signed on with Essex except for subversive reasons and that, short of this, the signing-on might as plausibly signify fidelity to a moderate line like Southwell's as any departure from Catholicism.

It is difficult, however, to believe that Donne was any longer an uncompromised Catholic when he became one of Egerton's secretaries. Egerton was not soft on Catholics[42] and would hardly have employed Donne if he had had any reason to doubt his religious position. He would have had no need to favour this particular applicant above others, for there would have been no shortage of suitable candidates for employment and there was no question of Egerton having loyalty to Donne's family or their religion. Donne must have seemed safe to Egerton, and this means either that Donne was by now some kind of apostate from Catholicism or that he was a crypto-Catholic for reasons of subversion or ambition. There is, however, no shred of evidence that Donne was, at this time or ever, some type of Catholic subversive.

The question of Donne and apostasy will recur later, but several points can usefully be made here. Donne's writings suggest a quick, vivid imagination and a strongly individualistic ego. They also suggest a being very much concerned with its own secular and spiritual salvation. So it is tempting to dramatise the issue of his apostasy in a way which stresses the loneliness of this individual struggle of conscience, rather as Carey does, the result being a version of the Romantic hero treated at the level of second-rate fiction. But it is important, without belittling the urgency of the issue for the individual (how do I achieve salvation? Or – more Calvinistically – how do I know that I am one of the elect?) to recognise that Donne's dilemma was a common one and that a number of solutions were possible, both for Catholics and Protestants. For a person of Catholic background, it must have been tempting, for example, to believe that occasional conformity was compatible with continuing loyalty to the Catholic faith or that mental reservation meant that a Catholic could swear to the Oath of Supremacy.[43] Integrity and interest might be made to coincide, or at least to be reconcilable, and if Donne's writings suggest a strong religious concern they also manifest powerful secular ambitions. The movement from full integration in a Catholic family to the deanship of St Paul's may have less to do with epiphanies than with a series of small shifts, compromises with circumstances which do not necessarily call integrity in doubt and which do not make Donne idiosyncratic. Within English Catholicism under Elizabeth it was the martyrs who were the eccentrics.

We simply do not know enough to probe very far beneath the surface of Donne's life up to 1601. Carey's attempt to do so is at least partially vitiated by his superficial grasp of history. The pattern of Donne's early decades is that of the typical gentleman-aspirant of Elizabeth's reign, with deviations at certain points (the schooling at home, the early arrival at university – though neither of these is unique to Catholics – the brush with authority when Henry was arrested) and it shows a young English Catholic, of mercantile family with genteel connections, seeking to be socially accepted as a loyal English gentleman. What degree of self-knowledge this involved and what tensions it created can best be examined in the early writings.

IV SATIRE AND ENVIRONMENT

Donne's early writings do not make up a single neat package. The evidence suggests that the 'Paradoxes', the verse satires, most of the elegies, some verse epistles, some lyrics, a few prose letters and 'The Progress of the Soul' predate Donne's marriage in 1601. Most of this work seems to be the product of Donne's time at the Inns of Court and just after, but we do not know when most individual poems or prose pieces were written and little can, therefore, be said about sequence. Some of the elegies may come after 1601 while, most importantly, the dating of *Song and Sonets* remains highly problematic.[44] Clearly, there are uncertainties which make it difficult to talk about matters like development except in broad terms, and these uncertainties cannot be resolved, in the absence of external evidence, by allusions or by stylistic analysis.[45] The safest thing to do is to treat the material as indicating how Donne was writing in the 1590s.

We need to consider, at the outset, who Donne was writing for and why he was writing. We tend to think of writing either in terms of print or of the highly private exercise of writing for oneself (although this is deceptive since many 'private' writers are, whether they know it or not, writing with print in mind). But for a writer like the Donne of the 1590s we need to rethink, for we are dealing here with work which is highly conscious of audience but not prepared for printing, even though it is not uninfluenced by what was being printed.

The basic audience for most of Donne's early writing lies within the Inns of Court. In Donne's time there these Inns, including the Inns of Chancery, constituted a sizeable community of around 1700 men – 'the largest single group of literate and cultured men in London'.[46] Among those who spent time at the Inns between 1590 and 1600 are a number of writers of interest in connection with Donne – Henry Wotton, John Davies, John Marston and Everard Guilpin – and it is clear that writing was a fashionable occupation at the Inns. It is also clear that, within the Inns, writers circulated work in manuscript among friends and fellow writers, and it is such coteries which provide Donne's basic audience.

The emphasis in Inns of Court writing tends to be self-conscious modernism. The most favoured poetic modes – verse satire and epigram – highlight a rejection or parody of courtly sonnet and lyric in a style which involves wit, obscurity and rhythmical roughness, together with an accompanying pose of scepticism and cynical rejection of the manners and values of Court, Country and City alike. Alert, independent of mind, aware of the latest ideas, the Inns of Court writer resists commitment to anything beyond himself and his coterie. His art is that of the young male in a position of privilege and potential. The potential leads to a second audience, for the Inns of Court existed in close proximity to the Court itself. Not only did the Inns entertain the Court on occasion but they provided many men who went on to distinguished careers in government. A social function of the kind of writing done by men like Davies, Marston and Donne was to draw the attention of the Court to the writers of the Inns, with the prospect of employment and/or favour. This possibility perhaps helps to explain the highly self-conscious role-playing of the satires and epigrams of the 1590s, with its emphasis on cleverness and free thinking.

Part of the pose of the Inns of Court writer, however, is of despising publication. Such disdain is rooted in the idea of the gentleman-amateur, and is thus linked with the 'superiority' of the Court proper, a distancing of oneself and one's art from ideas of writing as trade or commodity. In this connection, however, Donne is unusual among the satirists of the Inns of Court. Guilpin's *Skialethia* was printed in 1598, although anonymously; Marston's *Certaine Satyres*, together with 'Pigmalion's Image', came out in the same year, as did *The Scourge of Villanie*, both volumes anonymously; while Davies' epigrams appear as *Epigrammes and Elegies By I.D. and C.M.*, allegedly printed 'At Middleborough' in the 1590s. All three poets seem to have been members of the Inns when these works were published, but none formally signs his published work. Marston, of course, went on to work in the professional theatre (thus decisively forfeiting his amateur status) while Davies was published with Christoper Marlowe (the C.M. of the title-page) who was not an Inns of Court man and who was already working in the theatre in the early 1590s. Guilpin, Marston and Davies all break the code of non-publication even while using anonymity to preserve it. Donne, however, while participating in the Inns of Court modes of formal satire and epigram, avoids print entirely, the poems not being published until 1633. He thus sustains completely the role of the amateur[47] even though the printing of satires, epigrams and elegies in the 1590s indicates that there was an audience for such work beyond the Inns of Court coteries. It is interesting to note in passing, however, that Donne's work in these genres rarely alludes to the world of commercial publication and book selling which is prominent in the work of the other poets mentioned.[48]

In a sense the desired audience for Donne's early work is defined by the nature of that work. The emphasis on metrical irregularity in the satires, the use of detailed allusion, the wit, the rejection of notions of idealisation and fidelity in the elegies, the mockery of Court and City – these features work to exclude large numbers of potential readers. Adherents to high-Elizabethan culture, the uneducated, the old, women, citizens, workers are all alienated. Young, clever, ambitious, privileged males make up this audience, at least on the primary level, but there is also an eye upon what effect might be made on that part of a Court audience which might provide employment and favour. Being overseen displaying your wit to your peers could be advantageous, especially since this overseeing audience would include men who themselves had been at an Inn.

The writing we are concerned with here has, therefore, to be seen as both private and public. Donne clearly wants to be seen as private in relation to the public world of print, but it would be very misleading to see such writing as private in the sense of confessional or even intimate, despite the marked emphasis in it upon presentation of the ego. There is in confessional writing at least the pretence that the writer writes only for release, with no audience at all in mind, whereas Donne's work presupposes a coterie of like-minded readers. It may be intimate in so far as this is a small audience of men who know each other and share an environment, but the modes and manners of the writing largely preclude intimacy of the confessional type. Satire and epigram, in particular, strongly parasitic upon classical Latin writing, involve the knowing adopting of masks, the presentation of self in roles. This may, of course, be highly revealing (especially to those who know the codes) but not in a way commensurate with frankness, even though the relevant modes include the pretence of speaking with openness and without fear. Even the verse epistle, which Donne begins to use before 1601, is a genre with its own conventions, and although these include intimacy – 'Sir, more than kisses, letters mingle souls'[49] – Donne's verse letters remain highly self-conscious. Moreover, the Donne of the satires, elegies

and epigrams is, it was suggested earlier, likely to be aware of the
overseeing audience, and certainly the poems carry the sense of
an audience.[50]

The tones and manners of early Donne can conveniently be
seen in miniature in his 'Paradoxes', which seem to have been
written early in the 1590s. The editor of the standard modern
edition of these short prose pieces[51] provides information about
the traditions in which Donne is working and these indicate links
between formal literature and the exercises and disputations of
the universities and Inns. Donne thus begins his known literary
life with imitation, just as Ben Jonson said a writer should.[52] But
although this is exercise work it is nonetheless revealing in
relation to Donne's verse. In the first place, in writing 'paradoxes'
Donne is demonstrating his education and ingenuity, and is
participating in a fashionable esoteric genre. In the second, both
the material he chooses and his deployment of it relate to his
secular verse, while it should also be remembered that decisions
to work in one mode rather than another are finally, whatever
external pressures there may be, *choices*. In these prose pieces
Donne defines audiences, areas of interest and roles. Sincerity is
not to be expected, but indications of personality may emerge: 'To
be fantastique in yong men, is a conceitfull distemperature, and a
witty madnes'.[53]

'A witty madnes' naturally embraces paradox and the ingenious
presentation of problematic arguments. The more clever the arguments, the terser their articulation, the better; and the drive of
Donne's wit and his control over rhetorical figures work to outlaw
his targets, while embracing an audience of the like-minded.
Wisdom, it is argued in Paradox VII, is demonstrated by 'much
Laughinge' and this laughing wise man shows his superiority
over the courtier in vivid detail. He will laugh to see 'a gay man
leaning at the wall, so glistering and so painted in many colors
that he is hardly discerned from one of the pictures in the Arras
hangings, his body like an Ironbound chest girt in, and thicke
ribd with broad gold laces'.[54] The young writer will also show his
'conceitfull distemperature' by allowing 'some vertue in some
women'.[55] It is worth noting that the emphasis upon witty detach-
ment and superiority in the short prose 'Paradoxes' is still to be
seen a decade later in the prose 'Problems'.

It is, I think, significant that Donne, at the start of his career,
has chosen to use a witty, esoteric mode of minority appeal,

rather than established and widely accessible genres like the sonnet or pastoral. The chosen mode encourages the adopting of postures which subvert any obvious commitment to religious faith, the glamour of Court or the idealisation of Woman. Positions are, however, only lightly adopted, the mode encouraging the writer to be a chameleon. Consistency and sincerity are at a discount when wit and rhetorical flexibility are at a premium. The writer fits the mode, while the mode displays the writer in his 'witty madnes'. 'Fantasy' is a role played by intelligent and educated young men with time on their hands.

But Donne's main output in the 1590s is in verse, specifically in epigram, satire and erotic elegy, and such writing, at such a time, has to be seen as part of a group reaction against established modes, most obviously those of the sonnet and lyric. Such a reaction has social implications as well as literary ones.

Although high-Elizabethan poetry is not exclusively a Court product in the sense of being written only by courtiers, it can be seen as courtly in that Court is its focus. Not only does such poetry celebrate courtly ideals of behaviour but it is also commonly involved with the pursuit of favour and/or patronage. That part of it which is produced from within the Court is coterie work and thus parallels the poetry of the Inns of Court, achieving similar exclusiveness through specialised allusion and 'in' jokes. Its field of operation may include the creation of elaborate, distanced worlds (like that of *The Faerie Queene*) which are yet to be seen as hortatory versions of courtly reality and which may include a morally serious and critical dimension. In sonnets the field is more restricted, being commonly focused on a single love-relationship, one posited on the high valuing of Woman and intense consideration of the moral effects of love, the latter being seen in spiritual as well as physical terms. Such writing explicitly or implicitly excludes the mercantile and peasant as material: the genteel is where matter of worth is to be found, even though imagery allows the mercantile to return and the conventions of pastoral provide a function for the figure of the peasant.

Sidney's *Astrophel and Stella* was published in 1591 and the first three books of *The Faerie Queene* had appeared in the previous year. Sonnets were coming into print throughout the 1590s, the pattern being that the courtly product (Sidney's) is rapidly repeated by non-Court poets like Daniel (*Delia*, 1592) and Constable (*Diana*, 1592). The young poets of the Inns of Court reading such material would be encountering a popular product derived from the exclusive society of the Court and, in reacting against this kind of writing, these young poets are functioning both stylistically and socially. By distancing themselves from the sonnet and epic such poets are rejecting both courtly values and the popular aping of them, and this nicely combines independence and snobbery. Court is government at this time and the regime is deeply concerned to maintain its position by propagandising a monarchic and courtly mystique centred on the idea of hierarchy as an ideology divinely ordained for the fostering of the commonwealth. Translated into practical social terms this means propaganda for control of the state by Tudor monarchs, their nobility and gentry. To criticise and reject the art of this mystique can be seen as to criticise the mystique itself, even though the Inns were, at the same time, in the business of flattering the Court, and the critical implications of its literature are therefore frequently oblique. Snobbery comes in with the turning away from modes which have become democratised through print and their adaptation by writers like Samuel Daniel.

Subversion of high-Elizabethan art starts with parody (rather as the traditional revelry of the Inns parodies the rituals of Court itself). So we find John Davies producing his 'Gulling' sonnets and John Marston using sonnet form to introduce 'The Metamorphosis of Pigmalion's Image'. Marston's opening flaunts the antithesis of Sidneyan love while using the very form of that love:

> My wanton Muse, lasciuiously doth sing
> Of sportiue loue, of louely dallying.[56]

'Pigmalion's Image' itself can be read as a complex commentary upon high-Elizabethan ideals of love. Parody is a term that can be stretched to include the substitution of rough, harsh lines for mellifluity and the replacement of respect by cynicism and belittlement. At the level of literary models this pattern is repeated: Virgil and Petrarch give way to Martial (epigram), Juvenal and Persius (satire) and Ovid (erotic elegy), the displacement involving the flouting of conventional views of obscenity and the adopting of the witty, free-minded stances associated with such poets. Ovid was exiled and in Juvenal the satirist is one whose fearless frankness lays him open to danger from the establishment.[57]

The banning and burning of books at the end of the 1590s[58] suggests that satire and erotic elegy troubled the government, and several of the writers implicated were Inns of Court men. Donne is interestingly placed here, because as a writer of satires and elegies he is an offender, but the ban was on publication and Donne had not published. He is, however, the only poet involved in the 1590s in the vogues for satire, epigram and erotic elegy who is remembered by non-specialists today. Marlowe, who translated Ovid's elegies, is remembered chiefly as a dramatist, while Marston, Davies, Hall and Guilpin are little more than names. There are reasons for this which have little to do with literary merit, and to some extent Donne is the exception because of work other than satires and elegies. But there is little doubt that Donne found these modes congenial and that they fostered his talents.

This is not, however, really true of Donne's epigrams. Only twenty of these survive[59] and few readers of Donne remember any of them. It took Jonson to make something effective in English of the classical epigram. Donne clearly has the wit and terseness required, and he can do viciousness:

> Klockius so deeply hath sworn, ne'er more to come
> In bawdy house, that he dares not go home.
>
> ('Klockius')

The satiric epigram calls for concentration on its targets, the key pronouns being second and third person. It is not primarily concerned with self-analysis or self-presentation, although it can produce a strong sense of the poet's voice. Donne does not seem at home with the splintered pictures of epigram, but the brutality and callousness of 'A Burnt Ship' come easily and will be found again in the satires.

A proper understanding of these satires calls for them to be seen, in the context of other poets, as involving self-conscious participation in the type of reaction to high-Elizabethanism discussed above. If one reads the formal satires of Guilpin, Hall and Marston a fairly clear composite picture emerges, and an important aspect of this is self-consciousness. Thus Marston's 'Proemium in librum primum' to *The Scourge of Villanie* projects the poet in a clearly-defined role:

> I beare the scourge of iust Rhamnusia,
> Lashing the lewdnes of Britania.
> Let others sing as their good Genius moues,
> Of deepe desines, or else of clipping loues.[60]

And Guilpin's 'Satyra prima' exhorts his muse to fearlessness:

> No no, my Muse, be valiant to controule,
> Play the scold bravely, feare no cucking-stoole,
> Begall thy spirit, like shrill trumpets clangor,
> Vent forth th' impatience, and allarme thine anger:
> Gainst sinnes inuasions, rende the foggie clowde,
> Whose al black wombe far blacker vice doth shrowde.[61]

The poet wields the lash, abjures the epic or erotic role, is firm against sin and needs to be valiant. Moreover, the poet is fully aware of what stances he adopts, stances which suggest the isolation of the righteous.

The poses just indicated give the satirist a social function, this being defined further in the relevant poems. Marston cuts the satirist off from the poet who sings of 'clipping loues' and this distinction becomes satiric in 'Inamorato Curio' (*Scourge of Villanie*, VIII) when the poet attacks the conventions of the sonneteers, and Hall similarly distances himself from 'The loue-sicke Poet, whose importune prayer/Repulsed is with resolute dispayre'.[62] Since such love-poetry is coded into Court and its whole ideology, the rejection of this model of poet-as-lover has social implications: the satirist distances himself from the genteel-humble role of the lover and thereby from its social context. Instead he is an obvious power figure, flogging society's ills rather than being psychologically flayed by the obdurate mistress. And expectations of Woman have also changed. In *Amoretti* Spenser's lover-poet comes to see chaste disdain as a virtue and Sidney's Astrophel knows he should, but Marston, instead of seeing virtue beyond facial beauty and bodily grace, cannot penetrate an artificial surface:

> shee is so vizarded,
> So steep'd in Lemons-iuce, so surphuled
> I cannot see her face . . .[63]

and Guilpin's expectations are similarly of disguise and deceit:

> Thus altering natures stamp, they're altered,
> From their first purity, innate maydenhead:
> Of simple naked honesty, and truth,
> And given o're to seducing lust and youth.[64]

If courtly Elizabethan poetry associates courtliness with ideal and heroic behaviour (while remaining aware that vice is ubiquitous),[65] the satirists expect corruption and their role defines their personae as lonely in their perceptions. Women are seen as more likely to be whores than saints and the association of 'Court' with 'courtesy' arouses the contempt of Hall's persona:

> Fie on all Courtesie, and unrulie windes,
> Two onely foes that fayre disguisement findes.
> Late traualing along in London way,
> Mee met, as seem'd by his disguis'd aray,
> A lusty Courtier . . .[66]

Similarly, and in the same book of *Virgidemarum*, Hall sees in 'The courteous Citizen' only 'hollow words' and 'the great expence,/The fare and fashions of our Citizens', this latter to be seen as the empty aping of social superiors. The world the satirists anatomise is worth little or nothing. 'Thriving in ill, as it in age decayes',[67] it disgusts the poet, who takes refuge in disdain and fastidiousness:

> Fy Satyre fie, shall each mechanick slaue,
> Each dunghill peasant, free perusall haue
> Of thy well labour'd lines?[68]

Such superiority is comparable with the elitism of Court poetry, but Court is no longer acceptable, as the poet continues:

> Each sattin sute,
> Each quaint fashion-monger, whose sole repute
> Rests in his trim gay clothes, lye slauering
> Taynting thy lines . . .

Clothes no longer indicate the socio-moral worth envisaged by the sumptuary laws[69] but a flashy, valueless surface, while the integrity of the satirist can only be tainted by thinking about such Osrics. The poet's audience is now a narrow minority of 'free-borne mindes' which 'no kennel thought controules'. In these closing lines of 'In Lectores indignos' such fellow spirits are repeatedly seen in spiritual terms: 'diuiner wits, celestiall soules . . . sacred spirits . . . Heauens best beauties . . . blessed spirits'. Such language had belonged to virtuous mistresses and heroic knights, but those days are gone. For Hall, virtue belongs to 'the time of Gold' when 'men were men', whereas now 'the greater part/Bestes are in life'.[70] Guilpin, in his fifth satire, is driven to adopt the role of the solitary scholar:

> Let me alone I prethee in thys Cell,
> Entice me not into the Citties hell;
> Tempt me not forth this Eden of content,
> To tast of that which I shall soone repent.

This poet-figure is no longer wielding a whip, but has retired. The study is an 'Eden of content' and the addressee has the role of Satan, enticing, tempting the poet-figure to taste the social apple. Hell is the consequence of falling into temptation and a 'Cell' is Edenic. But 'Cell' is a double-edged word: the poet-figure needs the hermit's rural cell, but a cell is also a unit in a prison, and Guilpin's paradise is a retreat and an imprisonment, the need for which is created by the hell of the world outside.

The satirist, then, is alienated; alone or part of a small, righteous group. He sees hope in neither Court, nor City, nor Country, but survival may be possible in a bookish Eden or among 'free-borne mindes'. Yet the idea of retreat has to be a pose for the satirist since his material demands his presence. Guilpin's persona may long for his cell, but operates outside it, while the stock imagery of whipping and surgery calls for someone to be whipped or operated upon.

Marston and Hall are both extremely aware of their satirical roles and especially the scourging anger which these roles include, Hall's 'hote-bloodes rage' being typical.[71] The stress is strongly social: vice and folly are to be punished until they are obliterated, and society's health depends upon someone undertaking such a role. But it is striking that Donne, although his satires are strongly reminiscent of his fellow-Elizabethans in many ways, shows little interest in such a role or in the imagery associated with it.

Donne has the satirist's dislike of the contemporary (almost as a matter of definition) and this necessarily means rejection of Court and City. But his emphasis is not on administering the whip or knife and the most striking link through imagery with the other satirists comes at the beginning of Satire I:

> Away thou fondling motley humourist,
> Leave me, and in this standing wooden chest,
> Consorted with these few books, let me lie.

This is, of course, close to Guilpin's fifth satire and it is likely that
Guilpin has imitated Donne. In Satire IV the poet-figure speaks of
being 'At home in wholesome solitariness' (l. 155) and in both
cases the contrast is with the frenzy and superficiality of the
Court and town. Thus, in Satire I, the question which sets the
poem in motion is:

> Shall I leave all this constant company,
> And follow headlong, wild uncertain thee?
>
> (ll. 11–12)

At the poem's end the 'fondling motley humourist' has 'quarelled,
fought, bled', as a result of which he is forced into retreat –
'constantly a while must keep his bed' (ll. 110–12). Dragged out of
his study, as in Satire I, or importuned, as in IV, this satirist is a
victim rather than an hectic flogger or heated surgeon.

Yet, of course, such poses are ambivalent. The satirist as satirist
has to be out of his study, observing that which revolts him, and
the more vividly he records his observations the less convincing
his alleged love of solitude is likely to be. And Donne is vivid:

> She is all fair, but yet hath foul long nails,
> With which she scratcheth suitors . . .
>
> (V, ll. 74–5)

or, more famously,

> And though his face be as ill
> As theirs which in old hangings whip Christ, still
> He strives to look worse . . .
>
> (IV, ll. 225–7)

The satirist who sees himself as operating to flog, purge or
anatomise can claim public roles which necessitate his presence in
'the Cities hell' or in Court. Ambivalence may still enter the
relationship between satirist and material (as notoriously in the
gloating involvement of Marston's *Scourge of Villanie*), but at least
the satirist has reason to be present. Donne's personae adopt no
such roles and may even be aware of their own inconsistency:

> I had no suit there, nor new suit to show,
> Yet went to Court . . .
>
> (IV, ll. 7–8)

The invocation of the 'standing wooden chest' is interesting in this context. The basic figure is of confinement; the persona asks to be allowed to remain, in effect, imprisoned – 'and here be coffined, when I die'. The step from chest to coffin is short, and although this opening works to make a strong contrast with the world outside, the effect is curious: *even* this is better than the world of the 'humourist'. Better a coffin than hell. The 'statesmen' of his books may be 'jolly' and the poets 'giddy' and 'fantastic' but a 'standing wooden chest' remains steadily unappealing.

As satirist, then, Donne lacks a role of Marston's kind, or Hall's. The persona observes but does not consider reform, and where it is seeking something, as famously in Satire III in the religious discussion, the search is individual rather than social. Donne's satirist typically analyses and observes because he has failed to resist temptation and, to preserve a distance from the world, he scorns with such animation:

> towards me did run
> A thing more strange than on Nile's slime the sun
> E'er bred, or all which into Noah's Ark came . . .
> (IV, ll. 17–19)

The worlds of Donne's satire are vivid and alive. Another word would be 'restless', but it is worth noting that the personae themselves are also restless. The figure of Satire IV, as we have seen, notes its own inconsistency and the style of these poems is marked by rapidity: things are listed, pictures change, the focus shifts.

But in this restlessness there are recurring concerns, two of which are particularly striking. One is the Court, which is returned to naggingly as the example of corruption, condescension and folly:

> Nor though a brisk perfumed pert courtier
> Deign with a nod, thy courtesy to answer;
> As vain, as witless, and as false as they
> Which dwell at Court . . . ;
>   I (which did see
> All the Court filled with more strange things
>   than he);
>   (he being understood
> May make good courtiers, but who make courtiers
>   good?)
>   (I, ll. 19–20; IV, ll. 15–16; IV, ll. 151–2)

To some extent we should expect this emphasis in any Elizabethan satirist. Webster was to sum up orthodox thinking on Courts:

> Consid'ring duly, that a prince's court
> Is like a common fountain, whence should flow
> Pure silver drops in general: but if't chance
> Some curs'd example poison't near the head,
> 'Death, and diseases through the whole land spread'.[72]

The satirist is concerned with a poisoned land and, since the land is seen as having a 'head', the satirist must be very much involved with that. Nevertheless, Donne's emphasis is striking, coming to seem a genuine preoccupation rather than just one topic among many.

Even more noticeable is the attention given to religion. We are hardly likely to be surprised that a society in which religion was for many an urgent matter, which had seen a series of changes of religion in a matter of decades, and in which religion was intimately bound up with domestic and foreign policy, should be one whose satirists concern themselves with the subject. But religion surfaces almost obsessively in Donne's satires. It is, of course, the subject of Satire III, where the lines on religious truth are among the most famous that Donne ever wrote. The image is of strenuous struggle:

> he that will
> Reach her, about must, and about must go;
> And what the hill's suddenness resists, win so . . .

But we are moved on from this to something else:

> Keep the truth which thou hast found . . .
>
> (ll. 80–2, 89)

This movement is reminiscent of the contradictions between the satirist's desire to be left in his 'standing wooden chest' and his restless presence in a restless public world; but what is perhaps more important is that the formal religious concern of Satire III does not isolate this from the other satires.

In these poems religious reference often flirts with blasphemy:

> For better or worse take me, or leave me:
> To take, and leave me is adultery;

or:

> But how shall I be pardoned my offence
> That thus have sinned against my conscience?
>
> (I, ll. 25–6; I, ll. 65–6)

It may fit into traditional categories of anti-clericalism:

> Bastardy abounds not in kings' titles, nor
> Simony and sodomy in churchmen's lives,
> As these things do in him . . .
>
> (II, ll. 74–6)

It may use religious terminology for secular situations:

> my sin
> Indeed is great, but I have been in
> A purgatory, such as feared hell is
> A recreation . . .
>
> (IV, ll. 1–4)

or it may link fashion with the tortures of Christ as depicted in 'old hangings'.

A number of Donne's religious allusions in the satires relate specifically to Catholicism. So the condition of poets is 'poor, disarmed, like papists, not worth hate' (II, l. 10) and in the same poem words are said to have once had more effect 'Than when poor winds in our ruined abbeys roar' (l. 60). In Satire III, Mirreus is one who seeks 'true religion' at Rome 'because he doth know/That she was there a thousand years ago,/He loves her rages so . . .' (ll. 43–7) while in IV we have 'Glaze which did go/To a Mass in jest' and who 'catched, was fain to disburse/The hundred marks, which is the Statute's curse' (ll. 8–10). Such references are part of the texture of Donne's satires, worked in with other allusions, and it is their ubiquity which is striking, helping to define what is individual in these poems.

This individuality includes several components. Negatively, Donne avoids the imagery of flogging, purging and surgery. Positively, his satirist figures are at times hermits by inclination and yet restlessly responsive to social experience. The personae of Hall and Marston are certainly active, even hectically so, but their activity is, formally at least, purposive, whereas Donne's seem aimless – outraged perhaps, but without thoughts of reform. The restlessness, of style as well as focus, is also more marked in Donne because less easy to relate to a formal role. Finally, there is the frequency of references to Court and religion, spoken of above.

Such features should not be allowed to personalise Donne's satires too much, nor should they be too readily read back into his life. To an extent they arise as natural variants upon the situation inherent in writing satire as a new and self-conscious genre in England in the 1590s. The idea of the satirist as being hermetic by inclination has classical precedents;[73] by definition the satirist is socially disorientated or disaffected; and a concern with Court and religion is to be expected in an Elizabethan writer. The quality of Donne's satires, however, suggests that he found the genre sympathetic and the ways in which his stresses differ from those of Marston, Hall and Guilpin seem revealing.

There may be an element of social fastidiousness in Donne avoiding the imagery of the flogger and doctor. A young man with an eye on a gentleman's career might not relish projecting poet-figures of this kind, even in so formal a genre as verse satire. Positively, the figure of the satirist as studious and basically serious (the reader of 'grave divines' and 'Nature's secretary, the Philosopher' – though also of 'Giddy fantastic poets') fits well enough with Donne's known habits, while the restless anatomising of social life may project uncertainties which blur the seemingly confident pattern of Donne's early decades. Moreover, the quality of the best writing in the satires suggests that Donne is imaginatively engaged, and what emerges is a curious blend of the witty, superior satirist figure with another which is restless and unrooted.

Since satire is basically critical we should expect its references to the Court to concentrate upon its defects and, as suggested above, an Elizabethan social satirist is almost committed to take account of the Court. Donne seems more than commonly interested and there may seem to be a contradiction between this and the idea of the bright young man aspiring to a Court-based career. But we need to remember that the Court was a sizeable institution and that it was rarely united, being rather a collection of factions.[74] Donne was in no financial position to be a butterfly, and in seeking patronage and office it would be advantageous to present himself as a perceptive analyst of corruption and superficiality, and as someone whose independence and frankness would extend even close to the centre of power. The more serious, hard-working presences at Court (the Cecils, for instance) would hardly be displeased at such an approach, for only the most self-deluded would pretend that the idealisations of Court propaganda were mimesis of actuality. Donne's satire of Court can be seen as a finely judged approach rather than as folly or envy; while such an approach allows for the indulgence of the young intellectual's superiority over gadflies, vanities and fashion, an indulgence shared with his primary audience from the Inns.

Daring is fundamental to satire, the willingness of the satirist frankly to confront vice wherever he finds it being part of the basic stance. The young satirist in the 1590s could, so far as Court and religion go, draw on a very old native tradition of 'complaint',[75] modified now by adaptation to classical Latin models more suitable to the urban sophistication such satirists wished to present than a figure like Piers Plowman could hope to be. When Donne flirts with blasphemy, or strikingly links the secular with the spiritual, he is doing nothing new, since a touch of blasphemy belongs to the satirist's daring, while secular–social links merely reflect the interpenetration of sixteenth-century society. Yet, as we have seen, Donne alludes to religion far more often than Marston or Hall, and it is reasonable to associate this with his own religious position.

Donne had a difficult choice to make. Unbending adherence to Catholicism might mean execution, while deviance from Catholicism meant damnation – if Catholic doctrine was true. The only middle ways (a low profile, occasional conformity) were hardly compatible with Donne's ambitions or temperament. A low profile would scarcely be possible in the career Donne was preparing for, while occasional conformity neither faced the issue of damnation nor fitted the intellectually strenuous nature of Donne's mind.

It is, however, possible that Donne's position in the 1590s was essentially an intermediate, undetermined one. He was clearly on

course for secular, Court-based employment, and to that extent
headed towards a loyalist position not easily maintainable by a
known Catholic and not properly valid for a firm one. But a
decision was not imperative so long as Donne was a student
(although not proceeding to a degree was an acceptance of his
Catholicism) and even his military career with Essex would not,
in itself, call Donne's religious fidelity into question, except perhaps for extremists. In fact, such service could be seen as good
Catholic propaganda: 'See how loyal we are to Queen and Country'. And since the evidence is that when Donne felt he had to
make a religious decision he did so very conscientiously and
thoroughly,[76] it can be argued that the religious scepticism of the
satires is a device to postpone commitment. It should be added
that Donne may have felt in the 1590s that the position of English
Catholics was far from fixed. A change of regime was not impossible with a change of monarch; what would happen if Elizabeth
married a Catholic? Might some form of words be found which
most Catholic loyalists could accept?

Some such complexity of situation may help explain the nature
of Donne's references to Catholics in the satires. There is perhaps
sympathy in the impoverished, disarmed papists of Satire II, but
are they too contemptible for hate or is hate itself what is being
attacked? Is Mirreus admirable or ridiculous in turning to Rome's
'rags' because 'true religion' was at Rome 'a thousand years ago'?
'Rags' is scarcely complimentary on any reading and non-Catholic
readers could believe that Rome had been, in the distant past, the
focus of Christianity, but the passage seems carefully balanced.
Then there is the frivolous Glaze of Satire IV, trapped in his own
joke by the statute of 1580.[77] Here the interesting word is 'curse'.
Is the statute merely a curse for Glaze, or a curse in itself, and, if
so, in what way and with what tone? It could be read sympatheti-
cally with reference to Catholics, or, exploiting the more technical
sense of the word,[78] as endorsing the operations of the state and
church.

If the specifically Catholic allusions are taken in the context of
religious allusion in the satires, and if such allusion is taken, as it
should be, within the overall textures of these poems and their
personae, we have, I think, the impression of a risk-taking which
is carefully poised and finally uncommitted so far as religious
faith is concerned. These are neither the poems of a firm Catholic
nor of a decided apostate: and the lack of firm and final decision

fits with Donne's situation in the 1590s, with the kind of satirical persona that allegedly wants one thing but does another and with the witty restlessness of the style of these poems.

V   POEMS AND WOMEN (i)

In this section chronological problems are acute and finally irresolvable. By no means all of Donne's poems which are addressed to women or which involve them had been written by 1601 and, even if we confine ourselves to the erotic elegies and *Songs and Sonets*, we cannot say exactly what proportion predates Donne's marriage to Ann More.[79] It is highly unlikely that a poet would wholly abandon a topic involving at least half the human race so abruptly (although there do seem to be examples)[80] and it will be unfortunate if dividing a consideration of Donne's presentation of Woman into two sections, as will be done here, reinforces the old Jack Donne/Dr Donne division. There is no sudden break in 1601 and the structural pretence that there is, is only a convenient fiction.

Donne's treatment of this subject does, however, call for separate consideration because of the centrality of Woman in his writing; and the rise of feminist studies in our own time makes the issue raised by Donne's treatment the more pressing. The main reason for sub-dividing the topic here is that the social and literary forces which influence the way in which Woman is seen change considerably during his career, the main changes coming either side of 1601.

Very little can be said with any confidence about Donne's relationships with women before 1601. There are few references to his mother or sisters (perhaps because his exposed position as a Catholic made such references inadvisable), and only the most general suggestions about relationships with other women. The universities and Inns of Court were all-male societies, whereby sexual relationships with women of equivalent social and intellectual standing were almost ruled out (together with the chance to discover that women are not intellectually inferior to men). Such environments tend to encourage a dual view of the other sex: the excluded sex is both idealised and denigrated, the subject of chivalric dream and heroic fantasy, but also of pornographic sniggering and obscene enquiry.[81] All-male voyages with Essex's fleets would not be very different. Throughout the 1590s Donne's chief practical experience of women (family aside) was likely to be with prostitutes and women of socially inferior status. Contact with genteel women was probably slight and distant, since Donne was not in a position to have ready access to great houses or the Court, even though his career plans would, if realised, change all that.

Lacking hard external evidence we can only hypothesise on the basis of sociological probability – and Donne's writings. With the latter we need to be extremely careful, at least so far as the elegies and lyrics go. A very few of the latter may plausibly be associated with Ann More or the Countess of Bedford on grounds which mate poem and known external facts,[82] but most attempts to go further than this are merely sentimental. The belief that love is essentially monogamous is rubbish and so is the idea that promiscuity and erotic excitement are exclusively youthful activities (and so 'immature'). Any attempt, moreover, to decide on internal grounds which poems are autobiographical and which are fantasy is similarly doomed.[83] Anyone who writes poems and considers what the attempt involves knows that such neat categories are deeply misleading. Poems are inevitably related to the lives of their authors, simply because they are her or his products.[84] They may purport to be autobiographical or fantastic, but poems which purport to be autobiographical are selections, versions – and hence fictions – while poems which purport to be fantasy are nonetheless rooted in individual and social psychology – and so are biographically revealing. The personae of Donne's elegies and lyrics are sexually experienced. It is perfectly possible that Donne himself also was, well before 1601. If he was, however, we do not know with whom, how often, or with how many women he had made love. It is equally possible that he was a virgin,[85] fantasising on the basis of second-hand information and a vivid imagination. We do not know and it hardly matters, unless we want to treat poems as biography in a reductive sense.[86] If we are concerned with poems as energetic concentrations of experience the important and revealing thing is the poem, not its literal truth or lack of it.

It is also, of course, important to remember that writers are more often than not writing in known genres, and that it is in the nature of genres to define roles and attitudes which give the particular genre its distinctive identity. This at once creates difficult relationships between the writer and his/her own work, precluding simple associations between work and biography. If a writer works in the genre of the Petrarchan sonnet he or she is committed to the set of assumptions and images which defines that genre, regardless of the writer's personal beliefs and temperament. We cannot even be sure that success or failure in using a particular genre demonstrates commitment to its generic characteristics or lack of such a commitment, for such success or failure may as easily spring from talent or lack of it. Further, a writer may use the genre to subvert it (although even here the writer needs the genre itself) and the same considerations apply: the link between what is achieved and what is believed may be distinctly tenuous.

It remains true, nevertheless, that a consistent attitude or set of attitudes in a writer's work is revealing, perhaps of individual psychology, of social psychology, or of both at once. In the final analysis the adopting of one genre rather than another is a matter of choice, and revealing, however difficult the decoding of the choice may be. A glance back at the types of writing already considered can be used to make the point so far as Donne's versions of Woman are concerned.

In the 'Paradoxes', women have only general being. They are a category, as we should expect from the generalising nature of the traditions Donne is using. As a category women are objects for Donne's wit and of interest only in that respect. What happens is that male commonplaces are deployed and played with. So the argument 'That it is possible to find some vertue in some women'[87] is a *paradox* and the virtue argued for involves no real revaluation of Woman but merely the argument that characteristics men assign to women may be seen as virtues in so far as they are manifested in reinforcing the roles assigned to women by men: '... who can deny them a good measure of fortitude, if he consider how many valiant men they have overthrowne, and beeing them selves overthrowne, how much and how patiently they beare?'.[88] Here Woman's functions are to overthrow men and to adopt the missionary position. Later, in the 'Problems', the issue of whether women have souls, with all the objectionable intimations of male superiority, is similarly debated, to the conclusion that 'wee have given women soules, onely to make them capable of damnation':[89] men decide the issue – and decide to endow women with souls because women deserve the capacity to be damned. Elsewhere again, women 'delight so much in feathers' because they are vain and inconstant.[90]

Donne's satires do not concern themselves very much with women, even though satire of women is common in both the native and classical traditions.[91] But it would be misleading to see this reticence as suggesting respect for the feminine, for what attention is given to women in these poems fits her into traditional male-defined roles, as the 'plump muddy whore' (I, l. 40) or the cosmeticised, preened creature who, in Satire IV, interacts with equally vain men. When, in Satire V, Donne personifies the debasement of 'Fair Law's white reverend name' (l. 69) he does so by seeing it as 'strumpeted' and the same association occurs in II, when 'men which choose/Law practice for mere gain, . . . repute/Worse than embrothelled strumpets prostitute' (ll. 62–4).

Not too much should be made of these references. In the Paradoxes, Problems and Satires alike, the presentation of women is only one element in complexes which involve many other subjects, which are treated with the same confidence as merely objects for the deployment of wit. The most significant point here is simply that there is no sign of resistance: Donne accommodates easily to a line which sees women in roles defined by men and there is no evidence of any effort to get beyond these stereotypes. There is also no sign that Donne is preoccupied with women, whatever roles may be given to them. The personae of the satires are far more concerned with religion and the Court.

The position is very different when we turn to the elegies, as we should expect, given the nature of the genre. This is the classical erotic elegy, which exists primarily to express male attitudes to and views of Woman. It is male heterosexual verse, most directly represented in English poetry of Donne's time by Marlowe's versions of Ovid.

There is no reason why Donne's elegies should be consistent with each other, especially since their writing may cover a considerable period. But although, taken as a whole, range is one of their features, there are also similarities in the way Woman is seen in groups of them, this allowing for some generalisation.

One striking, even shocking aspect is the contempt with which woman is often seen. In Elegy II ('The Anagram') Flavia is described in a reverse catalogue of charms:[92]

> ... though her eyes be small, her mouth is great,
> Though they be ivory, yet her teeth are jet,
> Though they be dim, yet she is light enough,
> And though her harsh hair fall, her skin is rough ...
> (ll. 3–6)

and it is her unloveliness which, in the poem's use of paradox, makes her a good proposition for marriage, since she makes jealousy ridiculous and can be guaranteed to be faithful (the implications being that only unattractiveness can curb Woman's sexual appetite). Elegy VIII ('The Comparison') relishes the description of someone else's ugly mistress:

> Rank sweaty froth thy mistress' brow defiles,
> Like spermatic issue of ripe menstruous boils,
> Or like that scum, which, by need's lawless law
> Enforced, Sanserra's starved men did draw
> From parboiled shoes, and boots ...
> (ll. 7–11)

Julia, in XIII, is simply contemptible ('No poison's half so bad as Julia', l. 32); the lady citizen of XIV ('A Tale of a Citizen and his Wife') is gratuitously assumed by the persona to be sexually interested in him; and XV ('The Expostulation') opens with exasperation at Woman's infidelity:

> To make the doubt clear, that no woman's true,
>   Was it my fate to prove it strong in you?

The woman of I ('Jealousy') is a fool who 'wouldst have thy husband die,/And yet complain'st of his great jealousy' (ll. 1–2).

Woman in these poems is not only inferior but contemptible if ugly or resistant to the male persona, she having no imagined qualities except negative ones and being useful mainly as the object of male wit. Such attitudes are exemplified by the use of reductive images, as here in III ('Change'):

> Women are like the arts, forced unto none,
> Open to all searchers, unprized, if unknown.
> If I have caught a bird, and let him fly,
> Another fowler using these means, as I,

> May catch the same bird; and, as these things be,
> Women are made for men, not him, nor me.
> Foxes and goats, all beasts change when they please,
> Shall women, more hot, wily, wild than these,
> Be bound to one man, and did Nature then
> Idly make them apter to endure than men?
>
> (ll. 5–14)

Woman is not only bestial but is therefore an object to be hunted (that is her function and value) and valued only as sexually known and used. Elegy VII ('Nature's Lay Idiot') works similarly. Its persona instructs, almost creates the woman. The line 'I planted knowledge and life's tree in thee' (l. 26) mingles blasphemy with obscenity and leads to the closing burst of belittling imagery:

> Must I alas
> Frame and enamel plate, and drink in glass?
> Chafe wax for others' seals? break a colt's force
> And leave him then, being made a ready horse?

These poems create illicit contexts. In 'Jealousy' the sport is the adulterous deception of the husband; in 'The Perfume' the couple is involved in sexuality against restrictive parents; adultery is explicitly present again in VII and potential in XIV, while in XVI ('On his Mistress') the lovers are operating furtively in the context of 'thy father's wrath' (l. 7). Illicit love is hardly the invention of the erotic elegy, but its presentation here in terms of spies, betrayals and evasions, with the emphasis on wishing the deaths of others, works to introduce a sordid element which, in part, reduces further the status of the women presented.

Several elegies, however, offer views of Woman which are, it seems, celebratory rather than reductive, even though their view of love remains sexual rather than 'spiritual'. So in 'Love's Progress' (XVIII) the condition of Woman is valued in purely physical terms. Preference is equated with the valuing of gold and gold is valued in terms of use, with evident sexual overtones. Moreover, Donne's persona goes on to deny that Woman is virtue, beauty or wealth and offers a distinction between Woman and her properties which, in effect, leads him to offer the vagina as love's object in a way which defines Woman by her sexual organs:

> Although we see celestial bodies move
> Above the earth, the earth we till and love:
> So we her airs contemplate, words and heart,
> And virtues; but we love the centric part.
>
> (ll. 33–6)

The celebration of female beauty which follows elaborates this view, whereby human complexity is reduced to 'pits and holes' (l. 32). The view is finally pornographic.

Elegy XIX ('Going to Bed') does not involve such drastic metonomy. Here the woman at least remains the sum of her bodily parts, instead of being just one of them, and there is a rapturous erotic response to the imagined undressing and sexual activity which this prompts and releases:

> Licence my roving hands, and let them go
> Before, behind, between, above, below.
> O my America, my new found land,
> My kingdom, safeliest when with one man manned,
> My mine of precious stones, my empery . . .
>
> (ll. 25–9)

Three points may be made about these lines. The sexual rapture is that of the exploring male, but remains valid for part of what sex may be for both sexes. Yet Donne's poem sees Woman only in physical terms and his imagining reiterates male power over the female: the woman is to be 'My kingdom', 'My empery'. She remains essentially passive, to be discovered and explored – and the more precisely Donne makes language enforce this equation between colonisation and Woman the more firmly the latter is dehumanised.

The elegies discussed so far have in common a strong tendency to reduce Woman, to simplify human beings into objects of contempt, stereotypes, objects for conquest. But several are more complex, or at least less obviously reductive. So 'His Picture' (V) contemplates reciprocity: 'Here take my picture, though I bid farewell;/Thine, in my heart, where my soul dwells, shall dwell' (ll. 1–2); and much the same idea occurs in 'The Dream' (X), with the interesting addition that the male lover becomes the passive

element ('Makes me her medal . . .', l. 3), while 'His Parting from
Her' (XII) elaborates both ideas of mutuality and of a love which
involves 'souls' as well as bodies:

> Rend us in sunder, thou canst not divide
> Our bodies so, but that our souls are tied . . .
>   (ll. 69–70)

In 'The Bracelet' (XI) the poet-figure is the supplicant in a meeker,
more timorous way than elsewhere, and XVII moves from celebration of variety to the possibility of fidelity. Finally, there is the
strange 'The Autumnal' (IX) with its witty praise of age, which
ends:

> Not panting after growing beauties, so,
> I shall ebb out with them, who homeward go.

These elegies give Woman a more active role and are less
inclined to dehumanise her. But it should be added that they still
tend to present Woman as secondary, largely because the emphasis is upon the male ego, as is evident in the attention to the
weather-beaten, powder-marked figure of V, the vision of the
mistress imagining the lover's death at the end of XVI and the
first-person singular pronouns of the opening of XII. Also,
throughout these elegies, the mistress is constantly being exhort-
ed to be this or that, constantly being made by the poet's wit and
needs, allowed little autonomy or individuality.

Several things may be added. The first is that the contempt for
Woman in many of these poems is matched by contempt for
some categories of male – husbands, fathers and the lovers of
allegedly unattractive women. But contempt does not extend to
the poet-lovers themselves (except perhaps in 'The Bracelet').
These figures are witty, ingenious, self-satisfied: bright young
Inns of Court gentry, sure of their right to rule women's bodies
and of their superiority over mere citizens. Secondly, the presentation of Woman in the elegies is not idiosyncratic. The poems
amount to a brilliant projection of a very common male viewpoint
whereby women are to be denigrated (perhaps out of fear) and
also celebrated as objects for male gratification, to be shown off,
stripped and fucked. It is not for a male author to suggest a
woman's proper response to all this,[93] but its limitations as an

account seem very considerable, and what these amount to is revealed in a curious way by John Carey. Carey, when writing about women in Donne's elegies and lyrics, consistently uses 'girl' for 'woman', with no sign of self-consciousness, irony or criticism. I think Carey is right, in that the elegies, at least, refuse maturity to women, reduce them to 'girls', playthings, as against man (never reduced to 'boy'). But it also seems that Carey sees nothing offensive in this.

In a sense it would be trivial to trace aspects of this presentation of Woman to medieval anti-feminism, or to Ovid, or to Marlowe's versions of that Latin poet. Source-hunting is scarcely to the point when the offered version is so ubiquitous in male writing and thinking. And, if one makes the point that the sort of presentation we have been discussing is in marked contrast to the tendencies to idealise in high-Elizabethan literature, several comments need to be added.

The idealisation of Woman is not peculiar to Elizabethan writing. It has a long history and is rooted in the figure of the Virgin Mary. In secular love poetry it is developed within feudalism and in Renaissance neo-Platonism, most famously by Dante and Petrarch. In the Elizabethan period such idealisation is focused on the Court and this is particularly appropriate with a female on the throne. The reaction against such idealisation takes two main forms, the development of the erotic epyllion (*Hero and Leander, Venus and Adonis*) and erotic elegy, and the emphasis on the denigration of women in satire and epigram. These reactions are largely the work of young male poets, a number of whom are university and/or Inns of Court products, and they are part of a self-conscious rejection of prevailing fashions. It may also be the case that at some level they are reactions against the rule of a woman, especially one who would not marry (and thereby, in orthodox Elizabethan terms, be 'manned'). The limitations of Donne's sense of Woman in the poems we have been looking at thus have a socio-literary dimension, while, at the same time, they may, if Whitlock is right,[94] relate to a sexual education stronger on writing than on practical experience.

We should guard against over-simplifying the reaction against idealisation. High-Elizabethan writing was capable of being critical of Woman and of responding erotically to women's bodies,[95] so that a reaction can be seen as the development of attitudes which exist co-terminously with idealisation. Moreover, such idealisation can itself be almost as objectionable as denigration. Marston's 'Pygmalion's Image' extends an inclination in Elizabethan sonnets to see the idealised woman in materialistic terms and the enigmatic nature of Marston's poem catches perfectly the ambivalence of an idealising poetry which transforms human complexity into the simplicity of the ideal, and which elevates Woman as a kind of male gift. It is the male who puts the female on the pedestal or deifies her, so even when divine power is given we are reminded of who gives the power – 'I planted knowledge, and life's tree in thee'. Idealisation may be less obviously unpleasant than denigration but it is no more responsive to autonomy.

If it is a condition of individual and social maturity to be able to accept and respond to humanities other than your own or your sex's or your class's, Donne's elegies are not mature. The products of ways of thinking which see women as girls and girls as playthings or economic units, they are characteristic of a literature which is almost entirely male. More specifically, they are characteristic of a young male society in which true knowledge of Woman was almost impossible. Paradoxically, the elegies, in their brilliance, highlight the inability of their author to work beyond the boundaries of his society. Their value, then, is in highlighting, because of their brilliance, the offensive limits of their own vision.

2

1601–1615

I A BIOGRAPHICAL OUTLINE

'When Donne fell in love with Ann More and what first attracted him to her are now beyond conjecture'. 'Neither the exact date nor the place of Donne's marriage is known'.[1] So Bald, but although such basic information about John Donne's courtship and marriage is missing, the disclosure of the marriage ensured that its immediate aftermath is quite well documented. It is very clear that whatever marriage may have meant for Donne in emotional terms it was a disaster in relation to the career for which he had been preparing himself. His feelings for Ann may have blurred his judgement or his ego may have led him to feel confident that he could overcome any immediate loss of favour which resulted from his marriage to Ann. But Sir George More's reaction when he was told of the marriage, and Sir Thomas Egerton's reaction to More's complaints, destroyed Donne's carefully-built position quickly and, in a sense, permanently.

The reluctant father-in-law, Sir George More, was, in 1601, a substantial landowner at Loseley Park, near Guildford, actively involved in local affairs and a Member of Parliament in 'every Parliament during his lifetime from 1584 onwards'.[2] He had had nine children by his wife (who died in 1590) of whom five were female. Four of these married 'country gentlemen of wealth and assured position'.[3] Ann married John Donne, and Donne could have no reason to expect Sir George to be pleased.

We know that by the turn of the century Ann More was being brought up by Lady Egerton; that when the latter died in January 1600 Ann returned to her father's house at Loseley; and that she 'came up to town with her father' for Parliament in October 1601.[4] John Donne and Ann More were married secretly, around the beginning of December 1601, and Bald has plausibly conjectured that the wedding took place at the chapel in the Savoy, 'notorious later in the century for its clandestine marriages' and conveniently

close to Donne's lodgings.[5] The marriage was kept secret from
Ann's father (to whom she had returned after the ceremony) for
about two months. There is, I think, no need for elaborate
speculation about this secret wedding: the most obvious explana-
tion is that the couple were in love and knew that Sir George
More would not approve their desire to marry. The difficulty of
the situation was increased by the fact that marrying a minor
without parental consent, which Donne did, was 'a specific offence
against the canon law' and 'a serious breach of the social code'.[6]

When Sir George More heard, through an intermediary, of the
marriage he reacted by seeking to have the secret wedding
annulled, by having Donne imprisoned, by asking Egerton to sack
his secretary, and by refusing to provide Ann with a dowry. He
failed to get an annulment and Donne was only briefly imprisoned,
although his liberty was restricted for a time; but he was sacked
by Egerton, while More's refusal to make settlement on Ann must
have increased the couple's financial difficulties in the early years
of the marriage.

Material for the study of Donne's life between marriage and
ordination is much fuller than for the earlier part of his life.
Although the period between 1601 and 1615 is one of failure,
illness and frustration in relation to a public life Donne was
clearly an unusual man and one with connections with people of
social standing and achievement, so it is not surprising that
references to him and communications from him survive. Despite
this, however, and although we are told that 'Far more of Donne's
letters have been preserved than of any other English writer of his
own or earlier ages',[7] the record is far from complete, marked by
gaps, uncertainties of dating, and doubts at times about the
addressees of his letters.

It is not much of an exaggeration to claim that between Donne's
sacking by Egerton and his ordination in 1615 his life was a
failure. His marriage seems to have been a success of some kind
and he kept in touch with successful people. It can be added that
there were moments in these years when local successes occurred
– when Donne was able to travel with Sir Walter Chute in 1605–6
and with Sir Robert Drury in 1611–12, or when he received an
honorary MA from Oxford in 1610. But if we remember what
Donne's expectations were in 1601 it is clear that his position
throughout this period was weak in relation to those expectations.

Whatever solace marriage and paternity may have been (and

Donne's references in letters do not suggest that this was very great[8] there can be no doubt that his marriage not only broke his hold upon a secular career but that the relevant responsibilities made his material condition consistently fragile. Children came almost annually between 1601 (when Constance was born) and 1613 (when Nicholas was born) and in this period Donne had no permanent employment and no regular income from any source, except possibly a small annual sum from his father-in-law from 1606. The Donnes began married life apart and when they were able to live together it was first of all through the kindness of Francis Wolley at Pyrford and then, from 1606 to 1611, in a small damp house at Mitcham. Even when their living conditions improved through connections with Sir Robert Drury and they moved to Drury Lane (1612), they were living in dependence.[9] Donne also had lodgings in the Strand from 1607 to 1611, but this says more about his need to seek employment than anything else.

The basic picture of Donne's life at this period is hardly a narrative at all, but more one of stagnation, inaction; and surviving letters make it clear that Donne was fully aware of this.[10] But the passivity is erratic, even deceptive, for if lack of employment, the regular birth of children, depression, dependence and illness mark these years, they are also characterised by efforts to escape this condition. Such efforts can be seen, perhaps, on two levels, one of which is obvious: Donne's direct efforts to create and seize openings along the lines of his earlier career.

When Donne appealed to Egerton in March 1602 to re-employ him, he saw clearly that unless Egerton did this there was little chance that he would be able to resume the career which his secretaryship represented:

> To seek preferment here with any but your Lordship were a madnes. Every great man to whom I shall address any such suite, wyll silently dispute the case, and say, would my Lord Keeper so disgraciously have imprisoned him, and flung him away, if he had not done some other great fault, of which we hear not.[11]

Egerton did not relent and Donne seems to have accepted that this effectively destroyed for some years his chance of employment in or around the Court. He was not prepared, at this stage, to enter the Church[12] and was reluctant to go abroad, but the nearest he came to real employment between 1601 and 1615 was in his continental journeys with Chute and Drury. These provided breaks from domesticity and Donne may have hoped that they would lead to other opportunities. Certainly the impression one gets is of Donne progressively, if erratically, fighting back after the blows of 1601–2. By 1613 he was approaching Ker for office; we know that he actively sought secular posts in the last years before ordination;[13] and even his second period as a Member of Parliament (for Taunton in the Addled Parliament of 1614) can be seen both as evidence that some ground had been recovered and as a bid for preferment.[14] He seems progressively more willing to contemplate a move from secular to religious, for if the most depressing sign of Donne's dependence is his offer to write in support of the Essex divorce and the Essex/Somerset marriage, the production of *Pseudo-Martyr* and *Ignatius His Conclave*, together with the hints of his helping Morton,[15] indicate that Donne was willing to turn his hand to exploiting his reading in theology.

Reading, in fact, can be seen as the second way in which Donne resisted the pull to passivity. In itself the immersion in study can be seen as passive, a way of passing time, even a compensation for inactivity. But another way of seeing this is in terms of Donne utilising his quarantine by preparing for later emergence. This may have been unconscious. Donne was to protest that his study of the law was recreational ('my best entertainment, and pastime')[16] rather than vocational, and there is no evidence that he either practised or planned to practise law. But the study did keep that possibility open. His other main subject seems to have been theology. There is no reason to doubt that Donne's conscious motives here were interest in the subject for its own sake and genuine anxiety to resolve the matter of his religious loyalties. But it is also clear that he was willing to make material use of his reading at this stage of his life and that his theological studies fitted him for his eventual career in the Church of England.

In a sense, then, a narrative of Donne's life between 1601 and 1615 is misleading if it suggests a purposive pattern analogous to that of his first thirty years. The period is better seen as a baffled attempt to solve the problems created by his marriage. That marriage, its fruits and consequences, created the basic situation of these years, one which Donne seems able to see only in essentially negative terms. His efforts to overcome this are (at

John Donne

least in the surviving record) varied and largely unsuccessful, a circling around an unresolved problem rather than the upward curve which was the pattern and purpose of the earlier years.

II ASPIRATION AND FRUSTRATION

The ultimate object of Donne's career-drive was the Court and this, as we have seen, makes the satirical references to Court in his early writings ambivalent. With the Egerton secretaryship Donne was close to achieving his objective, only to be infinitely distanced from it by his marriage. There was, for some time, a physical distance also, with his main residence outside London, at Pyrford and then Mitcham, but the psychological distance must have been more important. Links remained because of Donne's contacts with people who were in favour at Court, notably Lady Bedford and Sir Henry Wotton; and Walton claims 'that both before Mr. Donne's going into France, at his being there, and after his return many of the Nobility, and others that were powerful at Court, were watchful and solicitous to the King for some Secular employment for him'.[17] But Donne failed to make up the secular ground lost with his marriage.

The 'Eclogue' to the epithalamion which Donne wrote for the Essex/Somerset marriage in 1613 is set in the country, which is seen as a place of solitude in a 'cold and decrepit time' (l. 3). By contrast:

> At Court the spring already advanced is,
>   The sun stays longer up; and yet not his
> The glory is, far other, other fires.
>   First, zeal to Prince and State; then love's desires
> Burn in one breast . . .
> The Prince's favour, is diffused o'er all,
>   From which all fortunes, names, and natures
> fall.
>   (ll. 15–19, 23–4)

The fiction of the epithalamion attributes much of the benevolence of the Court to the influence of the bride, but the traditional sun/monarch link blends with this. Donne, by way of flattering

Essex and Somerset, flatters the king. At this time he was hoping for help from Somerset, and he could believe that serving the favourite might do him good with the king himself. The remark about 'The Prince's favour' is poignant but also functional: if James heard of it, the hope could run, he might remember that his royal diffusion had not extended to John Donne.

The Court is also used as an image of the ideal on other occasions. So Elizabeth Drury is seen as the focus for paradise in the same way as princes are the focus of courts ('Second Anniversary', ll. 77–8); the ideal soul/body relationship in Cecily Boulstrode is that of a 'king and court' ('Elegy on Mistress Boulstred', l. 39); and Lord Harrington's virtue is such that 'I see/Death, else a desert, grown a Court by thee' ('Obsequies to the Lord Harrington', ll. 163–4). In the Essex/Somerset eclogue such views are developed into a full-blown eulogy, wherein the Court/Country antithesis is dissolved by the prince's power to 'animate,/Not only all their house, but all their State' (ll. 41–2). At James' court:

> . . . there is no ambition, but to obey . . .
> Where the King's favours are so placed, that all
>   Find that the King therein is liberal
> To them, in him, because his favours bend
>   To virtue . . .
>
> (ll. 79, 81–4)

This is almost sympathetic magic. Donne himself remarked to Lady Huntingdon that 'oft, flatteries work as far,/As counsel, and as far th' endeavour raise' ('To the Countesse of Huntingdon' – 'Man to God's image . . .' – ll. 51–2).

Clearly there is a strategic element here and we do not need to believe that Donne was as impressed with James as he claims to be. But Donne's writings show a marked traditionalist streak, so far as socio-political thinking goes, and the eulogy here may represent Donne's view of what Court and king should aspire to be. If James and his court were like this, so the coded line of thought runs, the writer's merits would be recognised. In 1613 Donne lacked both Fortune and Name; the king, through the court, could provide these. The sun/monarch as source of warmth/gold sums up well Donne's needs and desires.

Yet Donne might also be expected to show some bitterness towards a society where the realities were that an injudicious

action by a young man early in his career could result in disaster
through the reactions of older and more powerful people like
Egerton and More. If the conventions of the epithalamion direct
him to flattery of Court when writing of Essex and Somerset,
other occasions free him to exploit traditional scepticism about
Court. The eclogue itself uses satire of Court to point up the
alleged quality of James':

> Most other Courts, alas, are like to hell,
> Where in dark plots, fire without light doth dwell.
>
> (ll. 33–4)

In the Lincoln's Inn epithalamion courtiers are 'painted . . . barrels
of others' wits' (l. 27); in a verse letter of around 1608 to the
Countess of Bedford, Court 'is not virtue's clime' ('Madam,/You
have refined me . . .', l. 7); and in another verse letter to Bedford
we read:

> I have been told, that virtue in courtiers' hearts
> Suffers an ostracism, and departs.
>
> ('To have written then . . .', ll. 21–2)

Orthodox Elizabethan thought has it that a benevolent monarch
is state-paradise. But, by a simple reversal, tyranny is hell – and
tyranny put extreme claims for monarchy under great pressure.[18]
Given the supremely high expectations of Court – both materially
and in terms of ideals – it is natural that any failure to match such
expectations is magnified (as James' reign exemplifies). The split
in Donne's attitude is itself conventional, even while it represents
the division between 1601 and 1615.

This division must have seemed particularly acute for Donne in
relation to other men with whom he had contact, and especially
when these were men of his own generation. This can be seen at
its most extreme at a time when Donne must have been particularly vulnerable; the coming of James to the thone and what Bald
calls 'the consequent scramble for places' and 'an equally lavish
bestowal of honours in the spring and summer of 1603'.[19] This
process touched Donne at every conceivable point. His recent
employer, Egerton, became Chancellor and Baron Ellesmere; his
reluctant father-in-law, More, became Treasurer to the Prince of
Wales; his close friend, Sir Henry Goodyer, was made Gentleman

of the king's Privy Chamber. Among the coronation Knights of the Bath were Edward Herbert, Egerton's son-in-law Francis Leigh, and Edward Montagu, with whom Donne had sat for Brackley in Parliament in 1601. Others knighted at this time included Francis Wolley (who sheltered the Donnes at Pyrford), Sir George More's son Robert and sons-in-law Grymes and Throckmorton, as well as a batch of men Donne knew more or less well: Francis Bacon, Thomas Roe, Robert Cotton, Richard Baker, Walter Chute.[20] If these honours reminded Donne of what he had lost, the Court's progress in August must have exacerbated things, for the first night of that progress was spent with Wolley at Pyrford and the next two with More at Loseley. The pain and humiliation must have been exquisite.

Just how difficult these years were is perhaps best seen, oddly enough, if we consider the sources of consolation which existed for Donne. A desperate hope that something might break for him is perhaps one of these, and can be seen at work in the flattery of Court touched on above; but friendship is a more substantial factor. In a verse letter of about 1609 to Lady Bedford, in which Donne is consoling the addressee on a death, he uses a significant image:

> You that are she and you, that's double she,
> In her dead face, half of yourself shall see;
> She was the other part, for so they do
> Which build them friendships, become one of two.
>
> (ll. 1–4)

Friendship here is the reduction of two to the perfect unity of the One, with Platonic overtones and analogues in many of Donne's love poems. It is the same idea found, for instance, here in the epithalamion for Princess Elizabeth and the Count Palatine of 1613:

> . . . since these two are no more,
> There's but one phoenix still, as was before.
>
> (ll. 101–2)

And the idea is present again, more famously, in 'The Canonization':

> The phoenix riddle hath more wit
> By us; we two being one, are it.
>
> (ll. 23–4)

In a letter to Goodyer of about 1607 friendship is 'my second religion'[21] and to Gerrard in 1612 Donne says 'your friendship is to me an abundant possession',[22] possession being a telling word, given Donne's circumstances. At times friendship could dissolve distance completely:

> Riding I had you, though you still stayed there,
> And in these thoughts, although you never stir,
> You came with me to Mitcham, and are here.
> ('To Sir Henry Goodyer', ll. 46–8)

Here again we should see the theme and its articulation neither as wholly personal nor as wholly conventional. Friendship between members of the same sex was highly valued in the Renaissance, has deep classical roots, and was at times esteemed more highly than heterosexual love.[23] Donne's comments on friendship fit this tradition and, simultaneously, his own circumstances. He seems to have had a number of good friends, to have valued and kept them – Wotton and Goodyer being outstanding examples. In an early verse letter (?1597) to the former Donne wrote:

> Sir, more than kisses, letters mingle souls;
> For, thus friends absent speak.
>
> (ll. 1–2)

Donne was frightened by 'absence, darkness, death; things which are not' ('A Nocturnal . . . , l. 18), and we shall see these operating in his life at this period. Friendship's ability to cancel such nothings must have helped a great deal. But even as friendships consoled they must have reminded Donne of what he lacked, for, on the whole, his correspondents are people who have made their way, or are doing so – Wotton, Goodyer, Edward Herbert. It is a mark of the quality of Donne's friends, and also of Donne's own quality, that these relationships endure.

A second source of consolation for Donne in the bad years after his marriage may have been the marriage itself, but the evidence here is hard to assess.

The imagery of oneness provides a starting point. In orthodox Christian terms such oneness in sexual relationships should be expressed in marriage, as it is in Donne's epithalamia. The material and dynastic considerations commonplace in Tudor and Stuart marriage, however, together with the hierarchical system operating within marriage,[24] raise awkward questions about the practice of oneness, although the growth of a view of marriage as an equal partnership increased the chance of such a union.[25] Donne's own marriage only makes sense as a love or lust match, for it was both furtive and hazardous and neither party could realistically have seen it as materially advantageous.

The marriage of Ann More and John Donne brought disaster: temporary alienation of Ann from her father, loss of employment and prospects for Donne himself. Potentially, however, marriage also provided simultaneous consolations: sexual fulfilment, emotional reciprocity, companionship, children. But it is difficult to sustain any sense of Romantic Love in a cottage as one reads Donne's references to his married state (of Ann's we have, typically, no record). Instead, there is strain, guilt, a weary sense of responsibility. The blessings envisaged in Donne's celebration of the Somerset/Essex match seem far away and Walton's reticence may be significant. The version of Donne which Walton constructs seems to lead him to underplay the marriage. He presents it as founded on mutual affection – 'he (I dare not say unhappily) fell into such a liking, as (with her approbation) increased into a love with a young Gentlewoman' – but the telling parenthesis is picked up later:

> His marriage was the remarkable error of his life; an error which though he had a wit able and very apt to maintain Paradoxes, yet he was very far from justifying it.

Walton's most vivid anecdote is of Donne's vision in Paris of seeing 'my dear wife pass twice by me through this room, with her hair hanging about her shoulders, and a dead child in her arms'.[26] What this highlights is Donne's sense of guilt at having left his wife and family while he travelled with Drury.

A letter to Goodyer, probably of early 1607, illustrates the complexity of Donne's responses to his marriage:

> It is (I cannot say the waightyest, but truly) the saddest lucubration and nights passage that ever I had. For it exercised those hours, which, with extreme danger of her, whom I should hardly have abstained from recompensing for her company in this world, with accompanying her out of it, increased my poor family with a son.[27]

The danger and anguish of Ann's childbed are responded to but Donne sees his wife as needing recompense for the companion- ship she provides; the child is only an increase of family; the night of the birth has been an object of study ('lucubration') and an exercise of time. The response to his son's birth suggests a remark which Carey quotes from another letter: 'I stand like a tree, which once a year bears, though no fruit, yet this mast of children'. A tree endures, but this tree bears no real fruit (so the rich metaphor of 'fruit of my loins' is half cancelled); and the father displaces the mother as bearer of this annual crop of 'acorns, beech nuts and suchlike pig food'.[28]

Goodyer is also the recipient of another letter in which Donne uses the family setting not as his letter's subject but as its context:

> ... I write from the fire side in my Parler, and in the noise of three gamesome children; and by the side of her, whom because I have transplanted into a wretched fortune, I must labour to disguise that from her by all such honest devices, as giving her my company, and discourse ...[29]

There is the guilt of having brought Ann to 'a wretched fortune' (very different from those of her sisters), and as a result of this guilt there is 'labour' to hide misfortune from her by giving up to her the writer's 'company, and discourse'. The strain is striking, and Donne is writing to one of his closest friends. It is also Goodyer to whom Donne offers the picture of himself living in the country 'not in darknesse, but in shadow, which is not no light, but a pallid, waterish, and diluted one'.[30]

A decent sense of loyalty and responsibility may have stopped Donne from allowing marriage to become that dark nothingness which he feared, but it seems never to be the consolation and cherishment which the sun/prince of 'Eclogue' provides. Instead it is 'pallid, waterish, and diluted'. Without being cynical it seems reasonable to see Donne's tributes to his wife after her death[31] as recompense (which is not unusual after marriages which have failed to bring real oneness). It is striking that so little sense of Ann as a person in her own right exists: this lack of autonomy in the women Donne presents has already been touched on, and will be again. *He* is the tree which bears the 'mast of children'.

The darkness Donne writes of to Goodyer may have been his chief fear, and in his religious poems he often associates darkness with sin.[32] Although this is conventional enough in itself, Donne links the two with the appearance of deep conviction. But in the letter to Goodyer just mentioned, Donne defines darkness as 'no light' and the idea of nothingness which this suggests is connected in several letters with himself. So he ends another letter to Goodyer '. . . inifinite nothings are but one such; yet since even Chymera's have some name and titles, I am also Yours',[33] and Goodyer is also told 'if I aske my self what I have done in the last watch, or would do in the next, I can say nothing . . .',[34] while a verse letter to the Countess of Bedford – perhaps of 1609 – speaks of 'nothings, as I am' ('To have written then . . .'. l. 7). A nothing is a negative and it is close, in Donne, to stagnancy:

> When I must shipwrack, I would do it in a Sea, where mine impotencie might have some excuse; not in a sullen weedy lake, where I could not have so much as exercise for my swimming. Therefore I would fain do something; but that I cannot tell what, is no wonder.[35]

This is the voice of depression. Donne has, in this letter, just compared his enforced suppression of pleasure to being 'mine own grave', and his domestic situation to prison. This places him in a position analogous to the 'cloistral men' of 'A Letter to the Lady Carey . . .' who 'in pretence of fear,/All contributions to this life forbear,/Have virtue in melancholy, and only there' (ll. 25–7). Such darkness, nothingness, melancholy, are close to the sense of things running down which is basic to 'The First Anniversary' (1611) and which is touched on elsewhere:

> . . . now, when all is withered, shrunk, and dried,
> All virtue ebbed out to a dead low tide.
> ('To the Countess of Salisbury', ll. 9–10)

Even when life is not directly associated with running down it is seen as vulnerable:

> Th' earth's face is but thy table; there are set
> Plants, cattle, men, dishes for Death to eat.
> ('Elegy on Mistress Boulstred', ll. 5–6)

Death

> . . . doth . . roar, and gnaw, and still pretend,
> And breaks our banks . . .
> ('Elegy on the Lady Markham', ll. 5–6)

Donne wrote an account of suicide (*Biathanatos*) and says in its
preface that 'I have often . . . a sickley inclination' to it.

When speaking of depression in Donne's writings it is always
important to remember the conventional element. Several of the
quotations used above come from funeral elegies, while the
presentation of self as nothing in letters to social superiors is an
hyperbolic statement of a literal truth about addressee and writer.
But this does not explain the depression of private letters to
Goodyer, or the grim power of Donne's phrasing when he confronts melancholy, phrasing which suggests empathy rather than
a conventional pose.[36] We have, of course, seen that Donne had
good reason to feel frustrated and depressed – and, as cause or
effect, we know that he was physically ill on more than one
occasion in this period. The fullest account of one of these
illnesses is again in a letter to Goodyer (c. 1608) where he speaks
of 'a continuall Cramp', of gout and 'a Tetane'. Interestingly the
illness is something 'which I cannot name nor describe'.[37]

The personae of Donne's satires, elegies and lyrics tend to be
active and aggressive, far from the passivity and stagnation just
spoken of. But such passivity is only one part of the record of
these years. It is countered in part by the vividness of Donne's
writing even when he is speaking of dark or pallid moods, and it
is also countered by the efforts he made towards activity. The
figures of the satires, elegies and lyrics, however, are commonly
ones of domination and control, dismissing the sun, sweeping
away the relevance of Court, ordering the woman to strip, urging
a husband or father to die. But Donne's situation after 1601 makes
such attitudes hard to sustain and his self-projections are now of
being acted upon, by illness or dejection. Also, his position was
such as to make him a petitioner, which involved postures Donne
can scarcely have found congenial. This is not just, or even
primarily, a matter of penning direct appeals for help or
forgiveness, as Donne does, for example, in letters to More and
Egerton, but one of making himself available, of offering services.
So he writes to the Lady Carey and Mrs Rich from Amiens in

1611/12, not to ask for anything directly, but using flattery to keep himself in their minds: Donne's 'ecstasy/And revelation of you both' (ll. 53–4) is far from the historical record, but the gap between fact and fiction is ignored.[38] The poet who so often points to courtly corruption offers to write in defence of the Essex divorce and writes an epithalamion which transforms that divorce and its sordid context into the idealism of the court masque. The control which the earlier personae enact is a long way away and the figures of letters and funeral elegies are forced into awareness that others have the real power. A verse letter to Edward Herbert begins 'Man is a lump, where all beasts kneaded be' ('To Sir Edward Herbert, at Juliers').

One way of seeing Donne's life and art is in terms of the trying on of a series of roles to see how far they will fit the writer for society and a place in it. The early roles include those of the witty, superior satirist sharing his perceptions with a small, intimate group and hoping to be observed with approval by men of secular social influence, and of the male lover cuckolding other men, flaunting his brain and his phallus, dominating his women to the point of denying their autonomy. But in the period between marriage and ordination other roles are enforced. Instead of the woman being reduced to a satellite it is the writer who is cancelled in images of nothingness, and the swollen, caged husband imagined in Elegy I gives way to the coffined, imprisoned writer of the letters to Goodyer. Donne has to try out the role of penitent when writing to Egerton and More, and elsewhere the role of the grateful Petrarchan lover: 'Out from your chariot, morning breaks at night' ('To the Countess of Bedford' – 'Madam, You have refined me', l. 19). He is a lump to be kneaded or raw metal to be refined by Bedford (ibid., l. 1). He has to adopt subservient positions in place of truth and to outface unease about flattery by wittily extending it:

> If you can think these flatteries, they are,
>   For then your judgement is below my praise,
> If they were so, oft, flatteries work as far,
>   As counsels, and as far th' endeavour raise.
>   ('To the Countess of Huntingdon', ll. 49–52)

The roles, and the writings which project them, continue to relate to Donne's aspirations. Even when Donne is writing a weekly

private letter to Goodyer, the sharp projections of his sense of self
are calls for attention, and the adroit transformations of the
epithalamion on the Somerset marriage are a way of demonstrating
the poet's magic: 'I can make beauty, or anything, out of any
material'. The poet can thus be useful. As Bedford refines or
enlightens the poet-figure she is both flattered and reminded that
suns have function only if they have something to shine on and
that workers in metal need materials.

III TOWARDS ORDINATION

In 1601 Donne was secretary to Sir Thomas Egerton. He had
presumably distanced himself from Roman Catholicism and was
seemingly well placed for a secular career at perhaps quite a high
level. In 1615 he was ordained a priest of the Church of England
and in 1621 became Dean of St Paul's.

If one looks back from 1621 or 1615 over the years to 1601 it is easy
to think of Donne's movement to Anglican priesthood as a cynical
process or as the only way out for him from the position his marriage
had created. But it is necessary to see this process as dual. There is
no doubt that Donne was ambitious, or that it was made clear to him
that his ambitions would only be fulfilled within the Church of
England; and there is also no doubt that his ordination only
happened when it had become clear to him that secular preferment
was not going to come. But the record is one of integrity as well as
opportunism, and the two are not easily distinguished. It seems that
Donne could have been ordained to his advantage sooner than he
was and that some part of the delay was to do with his conscience.
Given that the England of the seventeenth century was, by our
standards, a society where faith mattered a lot to many, it would
have been foolhardy for Donne to have regarded religious choices
lightly. Damnation still meant something.

At some level and by some complex, largely hidden process
Donne managed to establish a distance between himself and
Catholicism.[39] He was intensely aware of the disabling effect of
his background:

> I had my first breeding and conversation with men of a sup-
> pressed and afflicted Religion, accustomed to the despite of
> death, and hungry of an imagin'd Martyrdome ...[40]

And when he wrote to More early in 1602 about his marriage he was aware that having loved 'a corrupt religion' was a charge against him. Catholicism here is 'corrupt' rather than false and Donne can write of its followers with sympathy ('suppressed and afflicted') but even in 1602 he can claim that the charge of loving the Catholic faith has been 'smoakd away'.[41]

It seems, in fact, as if a moderate religious position had a genuine appeal for Donne and that the form this came to take was partly defined by two particular reactions: to the Jesuits and to the relationship between church and state.

In *Ignatius His Conclave*, Donne repeatedly attacks Catholicism, and specifically the Jesuits, for being anti-monarchic. Ignatius 'found meanes to open waies, even into Kings chambers, for . . . executioners'; he is represented as saying that 'the name Monarch, is a hateful and execrable name to us'; he is canonised as one of the 'spirituall Butchers, and King-killers' who commend themselves to popes.[42] *Ignatius* is part of the controversy which surrounded James I's Oath of Supremacy, which many English Catholics were tempted to accept as a solution for their difficulties of conscience, but which two papal breves opposed with firm Jesuit support. This controversy reaches back beyond the Oath itself to the Papal Bull of excommunication against Elizabeth which had split English Catholics earlier.[43] Donne is writing on James' side of a controversy in which the king was personally active, and *Ignatius* is, among other things, part of Donne's effort to gain preferment; but his support for monarchy is consistent and sustained and it involves him in wanting close identification between church and state:

> . . . if these two principall beames and Toppe-rafters, the Prince and the Priest, rent asunder, the whole frame and Foundation of Christian Religion will be shaked.[44]

This, in *Pseudo-Martyr*, is precisely the view of the Church of England. Donne had demonstrated his loyalty to the Crown and state by joining Essex's expeditions of 1596 and 1597 but here his position is actively Anglican; more positive than Southwell's defensive line.

The Jesuits could only be seen as a threat to such a position. Within English Catholicism they were often regarded as disturbing elements well into the seventeenth century[45] and from an Anglican

religious and political viewpoint they were both perfect material
for propagandist appeals to chauvinism and fear, and for attempts
to divide and weaken English Catholicism itself. Donne might
claim that, as early as 1602, his Catholicism was 'smoakd away'
but it came close again on occasions. His mother, Catholic to her
death, returned to England with his Catholic step-father, Robert
Rainsford, in 1606, and that step-father was imprisoned in 1611
for refusing the Oath. The Catholic activism associated with
seminary priests, and with the Jesuits above all, threatened Donne,
reminded him of disadvantage, and pressed upon his patriotism.
The hostility to the Jesuits which marks *Pseudo-Martyr* and *Ignatius*
is scarcely surprising, and it typically blends the opportune with
the felt. But it should not be confused with hostility to Catholicism
at large. Both in poems of the 1590s and in remarks about 'a
suppressed and afflicted Religion', Donne establishes a neutral
tone which may shade into sympathy even while seeking detach-
ment.

Drawn by the idea of identification between church and state
and antagonistic to the rigour of the Jesuits, Donne defines a
moderate religious position for himself, even while his temperament seems basically other than moderate, and this position
happens to be close to that of the Jacobean church before
Laudianism became prominent.[46] Donne often defines, or looks
for, a position by making comparisons between Catholicism and
extreme Protestantism or between those and the position of the
Church of England.[47] Writing to Goodyer, presumably in 1609, he
comments on Barlowe's *An Answer to a Catholic Englishman*, an
Anglican reply to Parson's Catholic attack on James I's *Apology for
the Oath of Allegiance* (1607):

> In the main point in question, I think truly there is a perplexity
> . . . and both sides may be in justice, and innocence . . .[48]

Donne goes on to explain this view in relation to the Oath. In
another letter to Goodyer a similar irenicism is expressed in a
more personal manner:

> You know I never fettered nor imprisoned the word Religion
> . . . immuring it in a Rome, or a Wittemberg, or a Geneva; they
> are all virtuall beams of one Sun . . .[49]

He writes to an unknown Catholic friend:

> That we differ in our wayes, I hope we pardon one another.
> Men go to China, both by the Straights, and by the Cape. I
> never mis-interpreted your way; nor suffered it to be so, where-
> soever I found it in discourse.[50]

And to Goodyer again (1615):

> The channels of Gods mercies run through both fields; and
> they are sister teats of his graces, yet both diseased and infected,
> but not both alike.[51]

These remarks all come from private letters, three of them to
Donne's most regular correspondent. They all indicate the same
tolerance, seeing its absence as confinement (using the same
images which Donne employs for his own social state) and
religious differences as merely different vehicles for God's mercy
to flow like water or mother's milk. It is a position which suggests
a lack of interest in non-essentials and it is compatible with the
view that all churches have departed from one primitive Church.
It is also a view which, at least in theory, eases the problem of
choice. That it is not only a view which Donne felt able to express
to friends is clear, for example, in *Pseudo-Martyr*:

> My easines, to affoord a sweete and gentle Interpretation, to all
> professors of Christian Religion, if they shake not the Founda-
> tion . . .[52]

In *Essays in Divinity* he contemplates the idea 'That an unity and
consonance in things not essentiall, is not so necessarily requisite
as is imagined'.[53] Frequently when Donne writes of God he
avoids doctrinal statements almost completely:

> . . . turn to God . . .
> He will best teach you, how you should lay out
>   His stock of beauty, learning, favour, blood . . .
> ('To the Countess of Bedford at New Year's Tide', ll. 33, 36–7)

or, in another mood:

> So, to the punishments which God doth fling,
>   Our apprehension contributes the sting.
> To us, as to his chickens, he doth cast
> Hemlocke . . .
>   ('To Sir Edward Herbert, at Juliers', ll. 9–10)

But the remarks we have been quoting need to be read with some caution. They operate at a conventional level of abstraction, making space for themselves by distancing specific choices about doctrine and belief, seeking to allow a degree of latitudinarianism which the realities of Jacobean life did not always permit. The position Donne outlines is one which many of his contemporaries could accept in principle and which the Elizabethan and Jacobean governments could at times accept in practice.[54] But there were always limits, as there were to continue to be for a very long time, and the interpenetration of the secular and the religious meant that these limits forced choices in the physical world. So the Oath of Allegiance may largely be worded to facilitate Catholic acceptance, but it did not eliminate the need for choices to be made, and the Papal breves indicated this very clearly.[55] There comes a point when 'things not essential' need to be defined, and then the trouble starts.

Donne's moderation, on the evidence so far, can be seen as typically double-faced. In so far as it seeks to reduce the importance of difference and assert that mercy can flow along more channels than one, it can be seen as an attempt, at the personal level, to make religious choice less urgent. If 'the word Religion' need not be 'immured . . . in a Rome, or a Wittemberg, or a Geneva' then it is not vital for salvation to have made the only right choice, for there is no single right. Secondly, the sort of reasonable moderate view we have been considering would appeal to the Jacobean government, for it allows for religio-political stability, theoretically reducing the need for conflict between church and state, whether it be between Catholicism and England or between the English state and separatist tendencies within it.

But it is hardly surprising that Donne could not always keep the pressure of choice at such a distance. In Satire III the idea that there might be legitimate pluralities of viewpoint had been expressed with great urgency:

>   . . . will it then boot thee
> To say a Philip, or a Gregory,
> A Harry, or a Martin taught thee this?
> Is not this excuse for mere contraries,
> Equally strong; cannot both sides say so?
>   (ll. 95–9)

And in that poem Donne seems to advocate a pragmatic fidelity to the version of Christianity prevailing where you happen to live,[56] but this is done with a complexity and tentativeness which leave the famous passage on Truth effectively unresolved. Years later, the poet who opens a sonnet with 'Show me dear Christ, thy spouse, so bright and clear' can only resolve his questions by wittily concluding his poem with the paradox of Christ as faithful whore:

>   . . . thy mild dove,
> Who is most true, and pleasing to thee, then
> When she' is embraced and open to most men.
>   (Divine Meditations 18)

The more inward aspect of Donne's religious writing will be considered in a later section. For the moment what is important is to see the moderate pronouncements as one part of a complex whole and as part of a strategy designed to allow Donne to endorse, and finally to be ordained in, the Anglican Church. He does this, as we have seen, by actively taking the government position on the Oath, to the extent of writing *Pseudo-Martyr* and *Ignatius*, published documents in the Oath controversy. More specifically, he creates distance on the issue of martyrdom in the former text, seeking both to deny the traduction of himself 'as an impious and profane under-valewer of Martyrdome'[57] and to separate his endorsement of the 'glorious and triumphant Army of Martyrs' from the full Catholic postion:

> . . . to cal every pretence of the Pope, Catholique faith, and to
> bleede to death for it, is a sickenesse and a medicine, which the
> Primitive Church never understood.[58]

Here a reasonable, moderate position on martyrdom is firmly held short of fellow-travelling with Rome by the reference to 'the

Primitive Church'. As we have seen, Donne stresses the importance of agreement between church and state: *Pseudo-Martyr* acts
out this emphasis. Walton tells us that during the Mitcham period
Donne 'often retir'd himself, and destined some days to a constant
study of some points of Controversie betwixt the English and
Roman Church; and especially those of Supremacy and
Allegiance'.[59] What he endorsed was a loyalist position, and
unless we are entirely cynical we must accept that it was a
position Donne believed to be valid.

The story of Donne's movement to ordination is well known.
Walton has it that Bishop Morton tried to persuade Donne to be
ordained quite soon after his marriage and his account is the
more plausible for giving Morton knowledge of Donne's secular
ambitions. Walton represents Donne as refusing Morton's offer of
a benefice for several reasons, most strikingly uncertainty about
what his motives would be if he accepted. Walton comments on
the refusal that 'the heart of man is not in his own keeping; and
he was destined to this sacred service by an higher hand'.[60] That
higher hand might seem to be God; more immediately it was that
of the king, whose obdurate refusal to give Donne secular employment was matched by his willingness to provide religious preferment. As late as 1614 Donne was bidding for secular posts and
again became an MP.

It is not easy to find the right tone for writing about Donne's
religious life in this period, and especially about his approach to
ordination. In the abstract Donne might have sought the solution
of quietist Catholicism, moving far enough away from the Jesuits
to take the Oath of Allegiance. Or he might have become an
Anglican layman, avoiding controversy, living out the view that
religions should not be fettered. He might have found a position
between these, becoming an occasional conformer. He may, over
the years, have adopted any or all of these positions – but he did
not settle finally in any of them.

Walton, naturally enough, presents Donne as a man who
conscientiously thought and prayed until his path became clear.
In Walton's account, the delays work to Donne's credit and are
part of a progress to a saintly late life in the Anglican faith. A
more cynical account would stress the coincidence of ordination
in 1615 with the evidence that there was little chance of secular
preferment, pointing to the failure of the Addled Parliament and
the fall of Somerset.[61] Instead of being evidence of honourable

doubt and a scrupulous consideration of the priestly function, Donne's delays become evidence only of his clinging to hopes of mundane benefits. It could be pointed out that Donne's loftiest expression of the role of the priest in marriage:

> .. reverend priest, who God's Recorder art,
> Do, from his dictates, to these two impart
> All blessings . . .
> ('Epithalamion', on Somerset marriage, ll. 168–70)

was devoted to the cause of Somerset and Essex. The Donne who wrote *Pseudo-Martyr* and *Ignatius* was prostituting his theological expertise to Jamesian politics.

There is another kind of evidence which might be used to discredit Walton's account. We noticed earlier that Donne flirted with blasphemy in the 1590s: a number of his verse letters of 1601–14 show a similar tendency. So Bedford is told that 'Reason is our soul's left hand, Faith her right,/By these we reach divinity, that's you' ('To the Countess of Bedford', 'Madam, Reason is our soul's left hand . . .', ll. 1–2). In another Bedford letter the duchess is the object of the poet's 'pilgrimage' ('Madam, You have refined me . . .', l. 43). Magdalen Herbert's hand 'is/A miracle' and works as such on those it touches ('To Mrs M.H.', ll. 17–18). Bedford, on another occasion, is praised in terms of Christ:

> Though I be dead, and buried, yet I have
>   (Living in you,) Court enough in my grave,
>   As oft as there I think myself to be,
>   So many resurrections waken me. . . .
> This season as 'tis Easter, as 'tis spring,
>   Must both to growth and to confession bring
> My thoughts disposed unto your influence . . .
> ('To the Countess of Bedford. Begun in France
>   but never perfected', ll. 1–4, 7–9)

It can be argued that all Donne is doing in these letters is to use the hyperboles of conventional love poetry to flatter great women, which is certainly true in part. But these verse letters also show

Donne discussing God and faith directly and with seeming seri-
ousness, which makes it hard to believe that the 'blasphemies'
just mentioned are merely an unconscious use of traditional
devices, especially since Donne is usually a very knowing poet.

There is, however, no need to resolve the clash between
Walton's conscientious Donne and a more cynical version which
sees him as a time-server. This is only necessary if we are
committed to the sentimental simplicities of a J. B. Leishman[62]
and expect poets to be more 'sincere' and more 'consistent', less
complicated than other people. Donne is a maker of fictions and a
trier-on of masks, and this perhaps applies as much to his life as
his art. We have noticed several times how far roles and expressions of belief in Donne are typical rather than idiosyncratic. The
dilemma of his Catholicism is one example; the roles of satirist
and aggressive male lover are others. The Donne who, by Walton's
account, rejected Morton's offer of a benefice with anxious grati-
tude and humility is clearly not the same Donne who uses the
idea of the priest as 'God's Recorder' in the Somerset epithalamion
or who makes Christ's powers serve flattery of Bedford. But it is
disingenuous either to believe that any role any person adopts is
the whole person or that any role is wholly distinct from the
personality of its role-player. Similarly it is obtuse to deny that the
same verbal or physical action may serve more than one end.

The writings of this period of Donne's life are shot through
with references to fettering, imprisonment and graves. After his
marriage Donne was under great pressure, both to fulfil his
responsibilities to his wife and children and to satisfy an ego
which was aware of its talents and ambitions. The fact that others
knew he was talented may have increased the pressure, and the
whole situation is further complicated if we accept – as we should
– that Donne wanted to know and understand as much as
possible. In the circumstances it would be remarkable, and suspi-
cious, if Donne seemed consistent. The inconsistencies are to be
expected; more than just plausible. In depression personalities,
already complex, fragment. Donne is no exception.

A further point may be made. Much of what has been written
about Donne emphasises his individuality. This is proper enough,
backed both by the vividness and iconoclastic qualities of his
finest verse and by the evidence of his impact on his contemporaries. But we have also seen that Donne consistently tries out
conformist roles. These may be minority (the loyal Catholic, the

4

satirist) or majority ones (the loyal Anglican, the bashful lover) but they represent efforts to enact his famous dictum 'No man is an Iland'.[63] Put another way they are attempts to find correlatives for his individuality in society, suppressions of his ego which are yet expressions of it. Arguably the nearest Donne was to get to achieving this was the deanship of St Paul's. So long as we accept that Donne was a complex man, serious at the bedrock of his personality, we need not be surprised that he is both the scrupulous and respectful figure of the Morton interview (as recorded by Walton) and the cynical flatterer of Somerset. Bald has argued that Donne's behaviour in the Addled Parliament reflects both his loyalty to Sir Edward Phelips, Master of the Rolls, whose influence had seated Donne, and his links with Somerset.[64] This leaves Donne pulled between those keen to limit the royal prerogative and those anxious to keep the privileges of Parliament confined. The contradictory pressures represented here are thoroughly typical of Jacobean and Caroline politics, and at the same time of the pressures on Donne between 1601 and 1614.

IV WRITINGS: SURVEY AND MILIEU

In this period, as throughout his life, Donne is not a professional writer, certainly not if we define the term as meaning a writer who earns his or her living directly by writing. Yet the most immediately striking feature of Donne's output between 1601 and 1614 is its range and formal variety. In verse he moves from secular lyric to religious sonnet, from epistle to epithalamion to epicede, and in prose from the scholarly arguments of *Pseudo-Martyr* to the satire of *Ignatius*, from letters to friends and patrons to the detailed scrutiny of biblical texts in *Essays in Divinity*. The dating of Donne's work is too uncertain to allow much to be said about possible fluctuations in the quantity of his output, but what evidence there is suggests a steady application to his writing.

This range is not a new feature in Donne's life, but an amplification of an earlier tendency which now takes in new forms. By 1601 Donne had already worked in several verse modes; between 1601 and 1614 he attempts several new ones. But in this period he also writes much more prose than earlier, including two substantial volumes (*Biathanatos* and *Pseudo-Martyr*).

The forms that Donne works in during this period are significant in that the coterie forms of the 1590s – verse satire, epigram, paradox – give way to more public ones – epithalamion, funeral elegy, controversial prose. This reflects the realities of Donne's social situation. In the 1590s he is making his orthodox way towards secular preferment and his writing is partly a group activity indulged in for its own sake and partly a way of getting noticed by influential people. After his marriage, he is a supplicant in a very disadvantageous position whose talent as a writer is brought to bear on that situation. So much of the writing is now directed to specific events (the Essex–Somerset marriage, the death of Elizabeth Drury, the controversy over the Oath of Allegiance) and the range of the writing in part reflects the variety of demands which circumstances made on Donne.

This range is also interesting with reference to Donne's social position as a writer. The variety of Donne's output is reminiscent of the great professional writers of his time – men like Drayton, Daniel and Jonson – and yet Donne remains a writer who publishes, it seems, with reluctance, sometimes using anonymity to get the best of both worlds. The effort to have himself accepted socially as a gentleman (one who need not labour for a living)[65] seemed close to achievement by 1601, and in such a position a person could write as an amateur, the output being seen as part of a gentleman's expression of that cultivated, rounded situation and only indirectly, if at all, presented to the literate public at large. But in the period we are now considering Donne was forced back into the position of an outsider and a supplicant. His reluctance to enter the chuch may itself have had a social element, since the church was not a truly genteel profession. Writing was, in Donne's position, a way of regaining ground, but utilising his talent to such an end pushes him close to the position of the dependent writer, and this remains true despite Donne's efforts to distance himself from those who published.

Unease about being publicly known as a writer, together with a sense of being under pressure, are evident in Donne's work at this time. *Ignatius*, originally written in Latin 'between May and December 1610'[66] and quickly translated into English, presumably by Donne himself, appeared 'with no indication of the author or of the place and date of publication'.[67] The prefatory 'The Printer to the Reader' tells us that a friend of the author had written to him to say that 'The Author was unwilling to have this booke published, thinking it unfit both for the matter, which in it selfe is weighty and serious, and for that gravity which himselfe had proposed and observed in an other booke formerly published, to descend to this kind of writing.'[68] Such diffidence is hardly uncommon and is at times a fiction of the author's. The editors of Donne's *Selected Prose* tell us that Donne's authorship was 'known in court and university circles'[69] and, if we take this together with the anonymity, we have a situation in which Donne avoids any suspicion of vulgar publicity-seeking while gaining any credit that might be available in court circles. This allows for a kind of double significance in the remarks which suggests that *Ignatius* was an unworthy work beside this 'other booke' (*Pseudo-Martyr*). On the one hand there is the anxiety to be seen as serious and responsible, an anxiety again evident in a letter of 1619 to Sir Robert Ker when sending a copy of *Biathanatos*. There Donne says that 'It was written by me many years since', that he has kept its circulation very tight (it was not printed until 1646), and that 'it is a Book written by Jack Donne, and not by Dr Donne'.[70] In 1619 the concern to distance himself from pre-ordination work is easily understandable: the version of this concern which relates to *Ignatius* is similar but secular. But at the same time Donne demonstrates to anyone who knows his authorship of both *Pseudo-Martyr* and *Ignatius* that he is a versatile performer, capable of weighty polemic and of satirical prose turned to the service of king and country.

Reluctance to be seen in print is evident again in a 1612 letter to George Gerrard from Paris. 'Of my Anniversaries', Donne writes, 'the fault that I acknowledge in my self, is to have descended to print any thing in verse, which though it have excuse even in our times, by men who professe, and practise much gravitie; yet I confesse I wonder how I declined to it, and do not pardon my self'.[71] 'Descended' and 'declined' clearly suggest the vulgarity of print, something unbecoming a gentleman. More precisely, to print verse is improper for anyone of 'gravitie'. The language is that of the alleged authorial statement which prefaces *Ignatius* earlier. With the two Anniversaries the pressure to go into print is obvious enough. They commemorate the death of Elizabeth Drury, and Sir Robert Drury, her father, was a man whose support could help Donne. Drury, naturally enough, would appreciate public tribute to the dead child.

More intriguing is the evidence, in a letter of 1614 to Goodyer, that Donne was planning to publish a volume of poems. He writes that he must tell Goodyer this 'but so softly, that I am loath to hear my self; and so softly, that if that good Lady were in the room, with you and this Letter, she might not hear'. The lady is Bedford, and the news is 'that I am brought to a necessity of printing my Poems, and addressing them to my L. Chamberlain. This I mean to do forthwith; not for much publique view, but at mine own cost, a few Copies'. The word 'necessity' is then repeated, and the necessity is 'unescapable'. It has made Donne 'a Rhapsoder of mine own rags' and 'I must do this, as a valediction to the world, before I take Orders'.[72] The passage is fascinating and tantalising. The diffidence is clear, as is the sense of Donne acting under pressure. On the one hand Lady Bedford will hardly approve, but on the other there is 'necessity'. The act needs to be explained and justified even to an old friend, and it is carefully qualified. Donne will print, but 'not for much publique view' and not for direct profit ('at mine own cost'). What the necessity is remains unclear. The syntax suggests that this necessity extends to the dedication of the planned volume to the Lord Chamberlain, Somerset, and we know that by 1614 Donne was one of Somerset's clients. Donne had already written an epithalamion for Somerset's marriage. The natural suggestion is that the volume is to form part of Donne's clientage: that it had been suggested that Somerset might appreciate a volume of poems by Donne being dedicated to him. But this scarcely fits with the claim that 'I must do this, as a valediction to the world, before I take Orders'. It is difficult to see why anyone should force Donne to publish a volume of poems as a 'valediction to the world' or how a volume addressed to Somerset would operate in such a way. If Donne saw the proposed volume as a semi-public way of signalling his farewell to the world, why the business of Somerset at all? What is important, however, is the embarrassment, the sense of being caught up in a situation in which there is no socially acceptable way of acting. The uncertainty about 'necessity' may arise because Donne, who promises to explain the situation 'when I see you',[73] was under pressure from or concerning Somerset and deals with this distasteful circumstance by dramatising it as a 'valediction'.

The comments above about the range of Donne's writing between 1601 and 1614 and about his attitude to publication suggest some of the factors which go to define his audience at this period. But by comparison with the writings of the 1590s the situation with regard to audience is now more complicated.

We have seen that, in Donne's case, the idea of audience before 1601 means 'communities', and that the main audience for Donne is the élite community of the Inns of Court, with the overview of the Court proper. More precisely the core community is that of Donne's friends and fellow Wits at the Inns, while the Court element envisaged is made up of those who might patronise a bright young man from the Inns. Donne's reputation as a coterie writer in the 1590s establishes an audience which survives after 1601 and which could be a nuisance. This is the audience patchily defined by the early allusions collected by Milgate,[74] allusions which suggest that word gradually spread among people interested in modern poetry that Donne was a notably witty writer, and especially a satirist. The allusions Milgate has collected give Donne a semi-public audience and they underline his involvement with that interest in satire which, after 1600, could be seen as both subversive and tainted by association with the public stage.[75]

One way of seeing Donne's writing after 1601 is to consider it as involving an effort to escape from the image he had created in the 1590s. This effort has usually been discussed along the lines of Jack Donne and Dr Donne, with the ordained priest trying to lose the reputation so sharply etched by Baker.[76] But this cannot deal adequately with the situation before 1615.

Had Donne been able to develop the career which the secretaryship with Egerton indicated the reputation of having been an Inns of Court satirist would, having played its part in getting him noticed at Court, simply have fallen into place and his past, for his work for Egerton and later employers/patrons would have spoken for itself and marked him as an insider rather than a subversive. His letters to More and Egerton immediately after his marriage indicate that he knew the case against him, but this case only became a problem because of the marriage. As a result of the marriage Donne became an outsider and remained essentially that until his ordination. His effort to retrieve the situation involves him in defining his audience again and this redefintion further involves him developing a sense of several audiences, sometimes overlapping.

Two broad categories may help us get our bearings. The first may be seen as an extension of Donne's earlier university and Inns of Court years. It is fully discussed by Bald[77] and places Donne in the world of taverns like the Mitre and the Mermaid, in the company of such men as Sir Robert Cotton, Richard Martin, Christopher Brooke and John Hoskyns. The exact personnel and organisation of this company are not known, but what matters is that it includes other poets and is not made up of professional men of letters.[78] It is clearly a company of friends; it is a male grouping; and its literary component is informal and amateur. It should be added that its relevance to Donne's writing in this period is limited, at least in a direct sense. Such a grouping is important with reference to the *Songs and Sonets* (or would be if we knew more about the dates of these lyrics) and to the more intimate of the letters. But it represents a coterie which has more to do with Donne's writing before 1601 than after.

Another grouping is suggested by Walton for that period between 1607 and 1611 when Donne had lodgings in the Strand, 'whither his friends and occasions drew him very often, and where he was as often visited by many of the Nobility and others of this Nation, who used him in their Counsels of greatest consideration: and with some rewards for his better subsistence'.[79] This is not exactly an audience but is nonetheless suggestive of one since it presents Donne as a man worth cultivating, some sort of specialist, of value to the great in society.

The tavern-grouping mentioned above gives us, at least in symbol, Donne's basic audience – those people (all male) with whom he could communicate on equal terms, men like Wotton, Goodyer, Brooke and Gerrard. These men are those to whom Donne can mention the difficulties of his situation, to whom he can offer advice and consolation, and with whom he can exchange gossip, literary criticism and poems. The letters which are the literary product of these friendships are peculiarly suggestive in that they are not for publication and yet are not to be seen as wholly private either, for the letter (whether verse or prose) was seen as a literary form and its effects are studied rather than casual.[80]

Donne's letters, however, also give us a second unit of audience, that of the patron. This category is not wholly distinct from that of Donne's friends, for Donne is sometimes close to seeing Wotton as a patron and Bedford as a friend, but the difference is usually clear. It is a category where Donne is in the weak, or client, position, whether that is painfully evident, as with the letters to More and Egerton, or partially disguised by convention, as when he writes to such as Sir Robert Ker. Patrons, of course, are relevant here not only as recipients of letters but as dedicatees of more formal literature, such as the Somerset epithalamion and the Drury elegies. In such cases there may be a double audience – the recipients themselves, who may be willing to reward the author directly or indirectly if pleased with the product, and other readers, who might notice the author's versatility and wit, with possible advantage accruing to the author from this. 'Interest' is clearly the controlling feature here, and this means keying in to a restricted audience rather than the reading public at large. It does, however, place Donne among that large group of seventeenth-century writers who work within the constraints of patronage.

But Donne also, in this period, engaged in prose controversy, and this entailed publication either acknowledged, as with *Pseudo-Martyr*, or anonymous, as with *Ignatius*. This involves participation in a milieu which is both public and international, and is a long way from the élitism of satires and erotic elegies, even though the satire of *Ignatius* provides a link and there is élitism in joining the group of controversial writers. *Pseudo-Martyr*, in particular, is Donne's bid to present himself as scholar and these controversial works commit him to visible, inspectable positions which both group him among writers of controversy and place him, within controversy, among the public defenders of the national faith and polity as defined by the monarch himself. This, of course, means that *Pseudo-Martyr* and *Ignatius* can also be seen in the context of patronage. Walton claims that James 'commanded (Donne) to bestow some time in drawing the Arguments (concerning the Oath of Supremacy) into a method, and then to write his Answers to them',[81] the result being *Pseudo-Martyr*, while the Oxford editor of *Ignatius* suggests that that volume may have been sparked off by features in James' own contributions to the literature of the Oath.[82] Formally or informally, Donne writes these works as a man seeking help and preferment, and these works represent his fullest participation in public literature.

Another, rather evasive audience should be mentioned, this again being a group rather than an individual. A verse letter to Bedford is singular in having one formal addressee, but the existence of a genre of letter-writing in verse means that such a letter is simultaneously addressed to its formal recipient and to others who might read the letter as a contribution to the genre. In fact it is seldom if ever accurate to think of an audience of one in connection with Donne's work. We may be tempted to do this

with his religious lyrics, defining their audience as the poet himself
or God, but this is misleading. This is so partly because if you write
religious verse you are participating, whether you like it or not, in a
tradition and this entails a plural audience; partly because we know
that at least some of Donne's religious poems were sent to other
people (thus *La Corona* is dedicated to Magdalen Herbert); and
partly because the dramatic quality of the poems – and especially
their striking projections of images of the poet figure – forcefully
suggests awareness of onlookers who are neither just God nor just
self. This audience of onlookers may at first seem very general but
the wit and allusiveness of the poems in fact define an audience
which is exclusive in the manner of the satires, rather than inclusive
in that of the medieval religious lyric. At the same time, we should
not underestimate the degree to which the religious poems – or at
least the hymns and Holy Sonnets – belong to the puritan tradition
of self-scrutiny and are thus part of that process of self-examination
and restructuring which goes on throughout this period of Donne's
life and which leads eventually to ordination. Donne's most private
scrutinies have a social dimension.

It would distort and mislead to try to reduce Donne's audiences
of this period to any single milieu. Patronage and controversy
draw him into more traditional, more public modes than he had
used in the 1590s. Epigrams, erotic elegy and formal satire are all
essentially new modes in English verse in the 1590s and Donne is
among the first English practitioners of these modes, an élite
pioneer. But between 1601 and 1615 his main efforts are not with
this kind of novelty, nor in the radical developments of English
lyric seen both in *Songs and Sonets* and in the Divine Meditations.
Even if we regard a significant number of the former as predating
1601, and even if we accept that the bulk of the religious poems
precedes ordination, we are left with a body of work which, in
mass, is dominated by established modes: epithalamia, funeral
elegies, verse epistles, controversial prose. Yet this tendency,
enforced by Donne's circumstances, splits his immediate audience
along the lines indicated earlier, and if we knew more about the
circumstances bearing upon particular products we should almost
certainly see further splits. Perhaps the key text here is that letter
to Goodyer where Donne writes about the plan to issue a volume
of poems.[83] The complexity and self-awareness of the relevant
passage suggest a great deal about how particular and constraining
were the circumstances which define Donne's audiences.

Another way of examining Donne's milieux is in terms of how these operate to shape product. Such influences can be seen on two levels, which in fact interpenetrate – the generic and the social. A simple example is the epithalamion, in which the writer is generically committed to the celebration of marriage, the virtue of the couple involved and their suitability for each other. The act of writing an epithalamion thus commits the writer to a known or expected role, but this is also a role repeated as a social or even socio-political act if you write an epithalamion for such a marriage as that between Somerset and Frances Howard. Similarly, writing verse epistles to a great lady involves the presentation of that lady in roles of great power over the addressee which echo the conventions of courtly love even while they reproduce social realities in the lives of lady and poet.

So the Donne of the varied writings of the period between 1601 and 1615 is not to be viewed as one figure so much as a multiple made up of the interaction of personality with the shaping qualities of the modes in which he is working and the specific circumstances which bear upon his adoption of these modes and not others. The range of Donnes which emerges is quite considerable and involves the development of roles which are very different from the aggressive male lover of the elegies.

Most strikingly, the realities of Donne's social position mean that he is driven to adopt dependent roles in his writing. This is most obvious and direct in his letters to More and Egerton just after his marriage, in which he struggles to reconcile More to that marriage and to save or regain his job with Egerton; but dependence also drives Donne to create transformations of such women as Bedford and Magdalen Herbert, transformations which we shall look at in the next section, and to the excesses of the Somerset epithalamion. It may also be noticed here that the self-abasement of the poems to Bedford, for example, provides a parallel to that in the religious poems: the poet learning to subdue himself in face of the realities of adverse social circumstances is preparing himself for the self-humbling needed before God. In letters to friends Donne could relax more, while in a controversial work like *Ignatius* he could adopt the persona of the witty observer–commentator, but the recurrent need of this period is to offer subservient figures accommodating themselves to the postures of flattery.

V POEMS AND WOMAN (ii)

Milgate has usefully drawn together a number of early allusions
to Donne and his writings. Looking over the allusions before
1619, he observes how relatively seldom knowledge of Donne's
lyrics is revealed, when compared with references to elegies,
epistles and, above all, satires.[84] There are too few surviving
allusions for us to be very sure about what this might signify, but
it may suggest something of the challenge which Donne's lyrics
set, partly because they are more radically new than his work in
other genres and partly because they are individually and
collectively more complex. We lack the evidence to read them
chronologically; we cannot relate them to Donne's life in any
straightforward way; we cannot be sure when the first of the
Songs and Sonets was written – or the last; we should not expect
consistency; and we should be very wary of the term 'sincerity'.
Often, too, we need to acknowledge that nuances of tone are
evasive and, at times, irresolvably plural. Donne can be as enigmatic as Marvell.

Songs and Sonets was written at a critical distance from high-
Elizabethan sonnet sequences. Donne's lyrics are neither sonnets
in our modern sense, nor do they constitute a sequence in any
way comparable with *Astrophel and Stella* or *Amoretti*. In Donne's
collection the single focal mistress has vanished, to be replaced by
an indefinite number of shadowy shes (none given a name, none
a physical description) while the subservience of the poet-lover
has also disappeared, to be replaced by a more confident, more
demanding figure.

At times the voices we hear have much in common with those of
the elegies. There are, for example, notes of contempt for Woman:

> And when he hath the kernel eat,
>   Who doth not fling away the shell?
>   ('Community', ll. 23–4)

> Hope not for mind in women; at their best
>   Sweetness and wit, they are but mummy, possessed.
>   ('Love's Alchemy', ll. 23–4)

>   . . . for if it be a she
> Nature before hand hath out-cursed me.
>   ('The Curse', ll. 31–2)

But such notes seem, in a way not usual in the elegies, to be part of a contempt which includes love itself and even extends at times to the poet-lover. What I mean by this is that one of the recurring tones of *Songs and Sonets* is a scepticism about the whole world of love which amounts to a restless reduction of its aspects and attributes. So there is impatient rejection of constancy:

I can love both fair and brown,
Her whom abundance melts, and her whom want betrays,
Her who loves loneness best, and her who masks and plays . . .
I can love her, and her, and you and you,
I can love any, so she be not true.

('The Indifferent', ll. 1–3, 8–9)

Love may be 'Usurious' ('Love's Usury', l. 3), a devil ('Love's Exchange', l. 1), the cause of lunacy ('The Broken Heart', l. 1*f*). Moreover, this jaundiced, jaded response may extend to the poet-lover himself, producing the vindictive figures of 'The Apparition' and 'The Curse'.

Such restlessness is a key feature of these lyrics. Within *Astrophel and Stella* and *Amoretti* there is variety of attitude and emotional tone, but these are largely formally presented, as contrasts between sonnets or, if within individual poems, usually corresponding to divisions in sonnet form. Even in Shakespeare's sonnets, as first printed, the sense of variety is reduced by groupings which represent single dominant responses. We do not know if the order in the earliest printed edition of Donne's poems reflects the poet's wishes in any way, but it does, I think, represent the restlessness of the secular lyrics very successfully, extending our sense that this is an important feature of the individual poems. This strikes us if we come to these poems in the first edition of *Poems by J.D.* which Miles Flesher printed in 1633. The secular lyrics come late in the volume and are not printed as a single group (usefully making the point that kinds of verse in Donne should not be too rigidly separated). If we read Flesher in order, we reach the first of the *Songs and Sonets* after meeting elegies, verse letters and a number of religious poems, including 'The Litanie', which immediately precedes the poem usually called 'The Message' (which is untitled in Flesher). We turn the page from the petitions of the religious poem ('Sonne of God heare us

. . . As sinne is nothing, let it no where be') to an untitled account
of (we quickly realise) secular love gone sour:

> Yet send me back my heart and eyes,
> That I may know, and see thy lies,
> And may laugh and joy, when thou
>   Art in anguish . . .
>   ('The Message', ll. 17–20)

In 'The Message' the failure of love is marked by the play of the
pronouns, as 'I' and 'thee' act out their antipathy rather than
accord or unity. But 'The Message' is followed by 'A Nocturnal
upon S. Lucy's Day', with its sombre opening:

> 'Tis the year's midnight, and it is the day's,
> Lucy's, who scarce seven hours herself unmasks

and its extreme, almost parodic versions of the grieved poet-lover:

> . . . yet all these seem to laugh,
> Compared with me, who am their epitaph.
>   . . . I am re-begot
> Of absence, darkness, death; things which are not.
>   (ll. 8–9, 17–18)

In 'Nocturnal' we also meet another version of Donne's play of
pronouns. In this case the emphasis falls on the first person
singular in the two opening stanzas, only to give way in the third
to reminiscent plurals, with the isolated 'I' reasserting itself in the
fourth before the painful separation of lovers is stressed in the
final stanza:

> Since she enjoys her long night's festival,
> Let me prepare towards her, and let me call
> This hour her vigil and her eve . . .
>   (ll. 42–4)

It is 'The Message' rather than 'Nocturnal', however, that provides
the dominant tone of the early *Songs and Sonets* in 1633, as we
read successively 'Witchcraft by a Picture' (with its characteristic
tonal and argumentative twists), 'The Bait' (here untitled, a sar-

donic rewriting of Marlowe), 'The Apparition' (with its extraordinary evocation of sexual voracity) and 'The Broken Heart' (which has one of Donne's most strikingly violent openings) before reaching the famous images of lovers' unity in 'A Valediction: Forbidding Mourning' and 'The Good Morrow'.

I have chosen to illustrate something of Donne's variety by following the order found in the edition of 1633, but the point does not depend on this, for almost any sequence of six or more poems in almost any text of the *Songs and Sonets* could be used to indicate this highly important restlessness. The unsettled range of responses obviously suggests that the poet-figures of Donne's lyrics represent either a variety of responses to love by a variety of poetic lovers or various responses by a single figure, but, beyond this, the range suggests uncertainty about the nature of Love itself.

It is important to emphasise a curious aspect of this. Sidney, conventionally enough, tends to assimilate Love to Stella. She exemplifies Love, at times becomes it for Astrophel, and however far Stella may be the idealisation of Love and Woman as pedestalled product of the male imagination she continues to be a solid presence. Even where Sidney is most careful to insist that the 'real' Stella is a guest in the transient body (*Astrophel and Stella*, IX) the latter insists on its actuality. In Donne's lyrics, however, as has often been noted,[85] there is little sense of the female as body. There is nothing equivalent to the conventional catalogue of charms, or even to the anti-catalogue found, for example, in Shakespeare,[86] and there is not even the minimal definition which would have come with the use of a name or names (Stella, Diana, Delia). There are no names in Donne's secular lyrics, although there are plenty of personal pronouns.

Yet it would be inaccurate to say that Donne's lyrics disembody Woman, and certainly inaccurate to suggest a spiritualisation of Woman. There is often a strong physical presence (the 'poor aspen wretch ... Bathed in a cold quicksilver sweat' of 'The Apparition' (ll. 11–12), or the sense of a body in the bed of 'The Sun Rising' and 'The Good Morrow'); and even where there is no impression of female-as-body there is usually still a sense of the physical world, as with the objects which intrude in 'The Canonization' and the grossness of the opening of 'Love's Diet':

> To what a cumbersome unwieldiness
> And burdenous corpulence my love had grown ...

And, famously, Donne is a poet who does not deny the importance
of bodies:

> But O alas, so long, so far
> Our bodies why do we forbear?
> ('The Ecstasy', ll. 49–50)

Which leaves us with an intriguing question: What does it
signify, this recognition of the bodily which yet denies both
specific body and even a name to the women of *Songs and Sonets*?
It signifies, I think, two main impulses.

One of these brings us back to the restlessness noticed earlier.
Donne writes a secular love poetry which typically inheres in earth
while trying to escape it. This can be seen in the impatience with
category of 'The Indifferent', or in the attempt to move beyond the
confines of time in 'The Sun Rising', or in the riddling of 'Air and
Angels'. This may remind us of neo-Platonic orthodoxies, whereby
the bodily may be valued as a stage towards immersion in the
One,[87] but the restless tensions of Donne's lyrics prevent any
sustained or confident presentation of neo-Platonism. This is
perhaps most clearly seen in the poise of 'The Ecstasy', a poise so
fine that the debate as to whether the poem is a serious argument
for neo-Platonic views or a serious–sordid seduction device is
probably irresolvable (which is perhaps the poem's special, Marvel-
lian achievement). In this context, however, the important point is
that Donne's denial of specific bodily definition to Woman may be
seen as part of an attempt to overcome the clinging, reductive,
even frightening reality of flesh and earth. If we were more certain
of dating it might be possible to suggest that this is a reaction to the
failure of Donne's secular ambitions.

The second impulse seems to work in the opposite direction to
the first for, instead of being an impulse to dissolve earth
(specifically female body) into eternity, it works to assimilate the
female to the male. There is a recurrent aggression, an impatient
voracity, in the male personae of the poems. They attack, swallow,
sweep away, dominate:

> For God's sake hold your tongue, and let me love,
> ('The Canonization', l. 1)

> Whoever guesses, thinks, or dreams he knows
> Who is my mistress, wither by this curse;
> ('The Curse', ll. 1–2)

The personae dictate, exploit imperatives:

> Mark but this flea . . .
> ('The Flea', l. 1)

> Go, and catch a falling star,
> ('Song', l. 1)

> Let me pour forth
> My tears before thy face,
> ('A Valediction: of Weeping', ll. 1–2)

This impulse to dictate and dominate does not preclude a sense of resistant factors (rather, it necessitates such a sense) but it does figure an urge to overcome resistance by absorbing or at least governing it:

> She's all states, and all princes, I,
> ('The Sun Rising', l. 21)

Clearly, the denial of specific bodily Woman facilitates the enactment of this urge, even though there are cases where a refusal to be absorbed or dominated can only be coped with through the deployment of revenge and destruction, as in 'Community' and 'The Apparition'.

This does not mean that Donne's lyrics deny that Woman has autonomy so much as suggesting that the male personae resent that autonomy, or the idea of it. The urge to dissolve Woman's body is matched by awareness that Woman resists such dissolution: hence the tension in the poems. But the resentment, the desire to overcome or cancel Woman's autonomy, by ignoring specific body and by unnaming, means that *Songs and Sonets* is very much a male poetry of love and that there is a case for claiming that it is a male poetry about Love rather than about any woman or women. There is a striking awareness of variety in Woman, matched only by the awareness of variety in the moods and responses of the male personae, but the variety is resented more often than celebrated, contributing as it does to the unfixed, uncertain worlds of these poems. One aspect of this variety does include womanly qualities to be respected, even loved, as in the admiration of 'The Dream':

> Dear love, for nothing less than thee
> Would I have broke this happy dream,
>   (ll. 1–2)

and it would be silly to ignore the tenderness of which a persona is capable:

> Sweetest love, I do not go,
> For weariness of thee . . .
>   ('Song', ll. 1–2)

But even in 'The Dream' the woman keeps shifting, almost becoming Truth (l. 7), being mistaken for an angel (ll. 14–15), being seen as a torch (l. 27). And in the final stanza there is also a striking articulation of the poetry's inability to settle:

> That love is weak, where fear's as strong as he;
> 'Tis not all spirit, pure, and brave,
> If mixture it of fear, shame, honour, have.
>   (ll. 24–6)

The doubts expressed here recur throughout these poems, feeding back to our sense of the poet beyond the persona, but also reaching out to the inability to define the objects of the poet's attention. Donne is no poet of trust and Woman evades his apprehensions.

What all this means, I think, is that the *Songs and Sonets* constitute a great achievement, but of a kind which needs to be carefully defined. The poems add up to a various and intensely convincing expression of the evasiveness and chameleon-nature of love. They deploy wit, perspective shifts, tonal insecurity, nervously sensitive syntax and rhythm, brilliant phrasing and surprising collocations of imagery to create an art which is, in its playfulness, a remarkable version of an actuality. This goes to make ideas about sincerity and consistency dangerously over-simple and hence reductive. The truthfulness of the lyrics lies in their refusal to be consistent and in their conveying of the equal 'sincerity' in distrust, hatred, tenderness and lust. Inherent in this is a set of views and evasions of Woman which women may justly resent, since it denies their freedom and seeks to dissolve their beings into other things. But it is precisely here that their extraordinary value lies: that they convey so fully and with such artistic integrity (which is not the same thing as autobiographical integrity) such a various account of what love may be in the human male. This presentation may be of value to women because it is so revealing of the male, and to men not because it tells truth of women but because it tells disturbing truth of men. The brutality of the end of 'Love's Alchemy' is part of this truth:

> Hope not for mind in women; at their best
> Sweetness and wit, they are but mummy, possessed.

But this is only a part. The opening of the same poem has more to say in its complex of sexual reference, elision of Woman into Love and pudenda, and its sense of the evasive:

> Some that have deeper digged love's mine than I,
> Say, where his centric happiness doth lie:
> I have loved, and got, and told,
> But should I love, get, tell, till I were old,
> I should not find that hidden mystery;
> Oh, 'tis imposture all.

But Donne is often in positions in which he cannot afford to claim that Love is imposture. The non-specificity of addressee in the lyrics provides a fictional freedom: untrammelled by name Donne is enabled in the *Songs and Sonets* to release the full variety of his responses to love and women. But it is important to remember that these are also topics of other poetic modes which Donne uses – epithalamia, funereal elegies, verse letters – modes which force the poet into rather different kinds of fiction. In these modes Donne is writing to and for named people contemporary with him, people who have existence in history (usually at a social level superior to Donne's own) and often with the power to help the poet in his efforts to re-establish himself in society. Obviously enough, this situation constrains the poet, channelling the imagination into eulogy rather than satire, encouraging the fiction that perfection can inhere in the human.

In the case of Jacobean epithalamia the genre itself constrains a poet who uses it to present the bride in conventionalised roles which stress perfection while denying autonomy. In a sense, the point of marriage is to replace the autonomy of bride and groom by this new Oneness of the pair; but in stock Elizabethan terms this takes a form which fits rather neatly with impulses seen (usually in non-marital situations) in Donne's lyrics, for the standard stress is upon the giving of bride to groom, upon her subordination to him (backed by strong economic factors)[88] whereby the 'Oneness of the pair' may be no more than the male absorption of the female (Eve reinstated in the body of Adam). Since the epithalamion is a public form, concerned with the religious bonding of pairs in a social world, and a celebratory one, we are hardly likely to expect much individuality in the presentation of central characters. These become the role-playing Bride and Groom, and so the reader's interest is likely to be in how roles are defined rather than in the individual personalities of the role-players.

In 'Epithalamion Made at Lincoln's Inn' the refrain asserts that, for the female, marriage is that which perfects or completes her, making a woman of a girl – 'Today put on perfection, and a woman's name'. Marriage endows Woman with status: she is stellified ('our amorous star' l. 62) and is given a sun-like role and power:

> Thus thou descend'st to our infirmity,
>   Who can the sun in water see.
>   So dost thou, when in silk and gold,
> Thou cloud'st thyself . . .
>   (Somerset 'Epithalamion', ll. 149–52)

This may be linked with the power so often granted women in courtly lyric, while the association of Woman with Sun gives the bride a monarchic, even godly function. This is in itself a transformation in which role replaces consideration of individuality and, as usual, the power is given by the male poet, but it is also an apotheosis which is modified by the representation of other female roles in marriage. Perhaps the wittiest of Donne's epithalamia is 'An Epithalamion, or Marriage Song on the Lady Elizabeth and Count Palatine being Married on St Valentine's Day' (1613), and in this poem we have strong emphasis upon the idea of a new oneness, with the imagery of the phoenix and of 'one glorious flame/Meeting another' and becoming 'the same' (ll. 43–4). On this occasion the expected celestial imagery not only gives the bride a sun-role but riddles with the idea of the female and the male acting out role-swapping:

> Here lies a she sun, and a he moon here.
>
> (l. 85)

This is almost marriage as creator of hermaphrodites,[89] but the drive to etherealise the event is checked in this same stanza by the account of sexuality. The couple are:

> So just and rich in that coin, which they pay,
> That neither would, nor needs forbear nor stay,
> Neither desires to be spared, nor to spare,
>   They quickly pay their debt, and then
> Take no acquittances, but pay again;
> They pay, they give, they lend . . .
>
> (ll. 90–5)

The idea of sex as debt and payment has a long history, ranging from Chaucer's Wife of Bath to Victorian pornography, but it works here to anchor marriage in a sexual transaction figured as fundamentally economic, something which squares readily enough with the realities of Jacobean marriage and, specifically, with those of the socially and politically significant.[90]

When sexuality becomes central in the Somerset epithalamion, the realities of Jacobean marriage require the bridal star to fall:

> As he that sees a star fall, runs apace,
>   And finds a jelly in the place,
>   So doth the Bridegroom haste as much,
> Being told this star is fall'n . . .
>
> (ll. 204–7)

The fall is complex in its associations. Orthodox sexuality requires the woman, in Jonson's inelegant phrase, to 'fall upon her back',[91] while the falling of the woman may suggest Eve, and there is the suggestive decline of the sharp-edged autonomous star into the soft, amorphous, relatively undefined ('feminine') 'jelly'. Moreover, this fall has been anticipated, for in the previous stanza the bride had become a feast for the groom – 'Thyself must to him a new banquet grow' – this providing an elegant version of the brutal appetitiveness of the lyric 'Community'.

Sexuality and feasting are again associated in 'Epithalamion made at Lincoln's Inn' ('But in their beds commenced/Are other labours, and more dainty feasts', ll. 69–70), but on this occasion the feasting is worked in with the refrain-theme of marriage as that which releases the woman in the girl:

> This bed is only to virginity
> A grave, but, to a better state, a cradle;
> (ll. 79–80)

More interestingly, the feast modulates in the final stanza to a sacrifice:

> ... she a mother's rich style doth prefer,
> And at the Bridegroom's wished approach doth lie,
> Like an appointed lamb, when tenderly
> The priest comes on his knees t' embowel her;
> (ll. 87–90)

Here the bride wishes her disembowelling and her role is 'appointed' (by whom?), while the sacrifice is conducted with tenderness. Yet the 'rich style' of motherhood is only achieved through an image which makes a disembowelling knife of the penis and links the defloration of the virgin with the awful rituals of Elizabethan and Jacobean executions. The passage is disturbingly revealing, as the feast becomes gluttony and the alleged apotheosis of the woman becomes the violation of her guts.[92]

Genres which involve the presentation of real people necessarily include interplay between such people and the expectations associated with the genre in question. A poet can subvert these expectations, but only – as in mock-heroic – by creating a sub-genre: a poem of praise can hardly use satire of the addressee without ceasing to be laudatory. In fact, we expect such a poem to praise the addressee by representing her or him as fulfilling the ideals associated with the genre being used. This, however, allows the possibility of using negatives as markers. Poetry about Woman in the seventeenth century operates between poles represented by Eve and the Virgin Mary, and these inevitably encourage typification and dichotomy.

Donne's two 'Anniversaries' could hardly avoid transforming

their subject, the young Elizabeth Drury, since he did not know her,[93] and the poems are best seen as attempts to present Elizabeth as the embodiment of an ideal of womanhood. Other Donne poems which commemorate dead women operate along the same expected lines, and a common reference point is the figure of Eve. So the principle of 'ruin' 'made woman, sent/For man's relief, cause of his languishment' ('An Anatomy of the World: The First Anniversary' ll. 101–2), whereby the degeneration of the world is linked, plausibly enough, with the fall of Eve. Expectations of Woman are thus low ('Man to God's image, Eve, to man's was made,/Nor find we that God breathed a soul in her', 'To the Countess of Huntingdon', ll. 1–2) and this helps to define the virtue of individual women who escape the condition of Eve. The tragedy of Elizabeth Drury's death is that she had the capacity to offset some of the effects of ruination, but 'She, she is dead':

> She that should all parts to reunion bow,
> She that had all magnetic force alone,
> To draw, and fasten sundered parts in one;
> ('An Anatomy . . .', ll. 220–2)

The poem later recognises limits to this reforming virtue but reiterates its importance. Because of it, among other effects,

> Some women have some taciturnity,
> Some nunneries, some grains of chastity.
> ('An Anatomy . . .', ll. 423–4)

Similarly, Lady Markham, we are told, had the power:

> To have reformed this forward heresy,
> That women can no parts of friendship be;
> ('Elegy on the Lady Markham', ll. 57–8)

If Eve is cause of the Fall, a woman whose function is reformation operates analogously with the Virgin Mary, to save humankind by regaining paradise and thus heaven. So Elizabeth Drury is seen in 'Of the Progress of the Soul: The Second Anniversary' as one:

> Who made this world in some proportion
> A heaven . . .
>
> (ll. 468–9)

and the female addressee of the elegy 'Death' had achieved a similar, if more inward, reformation: 'Her soul was paradise' (l. 35).[94] The same point is made of Elizabeth Drury in terms of classical myth when we read that 'in all she did,/Some figure of the Golden Times was hid' ('Of the Progress of the Soul ...' ll. 69–70). Exemplifying the possibility of achieving such perfection, the versions of Woman which these poems present come also to stand for unity and harmony, virtues dear to Elizabethan and Jacobean politics. Without the virtue of Elizabeth Drury the corruption of the world is unchecked:

> ... a new Deluge, and of Lethe flood,
> Hath drowned us all, all have forgot all good,
> Forgetting her, the main reserve of all,
> ('Of the Progress of the Soul', ll. 27–9)

Without Drury's 'unvexed paradise' ('An Anatomy ...' l. 363) everything is in chaos.

Such women are important because exemplary and they are unsurprisingly figured as jewels. In 'A Funeral Elegy' Drury is 'pearls, and rubies' (l. 5); Markham is 'diamonds, rubies, sapphires, pearls ...' (l. 24); and the woman of 'Elegy: Death' is 'sapphirine, and clear' (l. 21). Such imagery draws on both biblical and secular traditions,[95] stressing moral and, with Drury, sexual purity in ways which draw the subjects away from Eve and towards the Virgin Mary. From this it is only a short step to that praise of individual women through explicitly religious language which we find in several of Donne's verse letters. The Countess of Bedford is equated with divinity:

> Reason is our soul's left hand, Faith her right,
> By these we reach divinity, that's you;
> ('To the Countess of Bedford', ll. 1–2)

and this association is elaborated throughout the poem, with Bedford becoming the poet's icon. In another Bedford poem the poet-figure becomes a pilgrim:

> So in this pilgrimage I would behold
> You as you're Virtue's temple ...
> ('To the Countess of Bedford', 'You have refined me', ll. 43–4)

and 'A Letter to the Lady Carey . . .' is shot through with religious terms (saints, schism, convertite, apostleship, cloisteral, revelation).

The distance between Woman as 'but mummy, possessed' ('Love's Alchemy' l. 24) and 'Virtue's temple' is, of course, enormous; as great as that between Eve (possessed by Satan) and the Virgin Mary (her womb occupied by the Saviour). It is obvious that Woman as Eve is most prominent in *Songs and Sonets*, erotic elegies and satires, while Woman as Mary predominates in epithalamia, funereal elegies and verse letters. This distinction is made more suggestive when it is noted that it is only in the latter categories that the women acquire names. If, broadly speaking, Donne only praises women's moral qualities when he is addressing a named woman it is tempting to see his praise of Woman as largely flattery and, on the other hand, to feel that the venom of 'The Progress of the Soul' or the erotic admiration of Elegy XIX represents the poet's true feelings. Such clearcut distinctions are, however, deceptive.

In all these poems generic considerations play a part, and in every case such considerations militate against simple possibilities of sincerity. It is to be expected that Woman in epithalamia and funereal elegy will be praised for moral virtue, that Woman in erotic elegy will be praised for sexual attractiveness, and that Woman in satire will exemplify viciousness and depravity. *Songs and Sonets* may seem to be an exception, in that generic expectations that Woman is praised in lyric collections are only intermittently fulfilled, but Donne is, in fact, developing an enigmatic mixed lyric tradition, drawing praise and satire together in a way which reaches back to Wyatt and is consistent with that European lyric tradition discussed by Guss.[96] Obviously when, as in epithalamia and funereal elegy, generic considerations unite with matters of patronage and the naming of important public figures, the constraints upon a poet in Donne's dependent position are made more evident than in lyric or erotic elegy, but it would be dangerously naive to press this contrast very far. Donne, as writer of erotic verse, is not operating privately: the poems are shaped as they are to impress a predominantly male audience with the poet's wit, sophistication and intelligence, in ways which make the poems – whatever else they may be – documents in Donne's struggle for a career.

Both generic considerations and material ones tell against the possibility of any single poem or type of poem expressing Donne's true view of Woman (even if we find it credible that he ever had a single view) or, indeed, of any individual woman. The test of quality does not help, either for the simple reason that Donne can write with equal conviction whether satirising or praising. It may be better to regard the variety of response as itself the truth and to accept that Donne's imagination involves 'sincere' commitment, however momentary, to all the responses articulated in the poems. And we might then note that these responses figure Woman as a paradox and as weighted with responsibility.

The paradox is inherent in the Eve/Mary dichotomy and is perhaps most fully articulated in a verse letter to the Countess of Huntingdon, 'Madam,/Man in God's image, Eve, to man's was made' (?1608–9). Here expectations of Woman are low and thus:

> In woman so perchance mild innocence
> A seldom comet is, but active good
> A miracle, which reason 'scapes, and sense . . .

Yet virtue is to be found in the countess. Therefore:

> If the world's age, and death be argued well
>   By the sun's fall, which now towards earth doth bend,
> Then we might fear that virtue, since she fell
>   So low as woman, should be near her end.

But this is untrue:

> . . . she's not stopped, but raised; exiled by men
> She fled to heaven, that's heavenly things, that's you . . .

Virtue 'gilded' men 'but you are gold, and she' (ll. 9–11, 17–20, 21–2, 25). Woman is seen as inferior to Man, but also superior and the paradox is doubled, since virtue is itself female. So long as womanhood is figured in terms of Eve and Mary, Woman is a paradox, only comprehensible when individuals are presented as either one or the other, puzzling and disturbing when both, since the theological displacement of the one by the other is validated in a fallen world only by exceptional women who regain paradise or restore the Golden Age.

Woman's responsibility is clear enough, if again paradoxical. As Eve she engineers the Fall. Analogically, she has responsibility, therefore, to aspire to the condition of the Virgin Mary so that the consequences of the Fall may be cancelled. There is, of course, a parallel account of Man, by which Adam, Eve's senior in creation and relation to God, is responsible for her and thus for the Fall, and by which salvation is the function of the second Adam, Christ. But the male-dominated traditions of Christian medieval and Renaissance culture dwell mainly on Eve's role in the Fall,[97] while Mariolatory, the emphasis upon the figure of Elizabeth I (nicely counterpointed by Mary I and Mary of Scots), and the stress in Renaissance love poetry on the mistress' responsibility for the welfare of the poet-lover, all underline the strong appeal, for males, of making Woman responsible for making salvation possible (which is, after all, logical if Woman has caused the Fall anyway). Since Eve allowed the serpent to possess her it is only proper that Mary should admit the Holy Spirit so that Christ can fulfil his mission. In the world of epithalamia this is acted out in themes of marital chastity and with the image of the phallic knife.

What follows, I think, from all this is that there is a consistent urge in Donne's woman-focused poetry to categorise Woman, an urge which, however, is undercut by the subjects' refusal to become singular, this singularity being also denied by the simultaneous presence of dual categories which cannot be reconciled. Donne, often brilliantly, articulates a range of possibilities for Woman, but he remains firmly within a male position, one which cannot release her from the dual challenge of Eve and Mary, cannot envisage her in social roles except those allowed by male-dominated societies, and cannot avoid seeking to control her by bestowing roles upon her. Arguably it is as much an imposition to stellify, or even deify, as it is to denigrate or withhold a soul. It would be a mistake to isolate Donne in this respect, in exactly the way in which it would be an error to isolate Ben Jonson because of his political conservatism. Both men are typical at heart. What is significant is that both embody something which amounts to criticism of the orthodoxy. In the case of Donne's poetry of Woman it is the disturbancy and inconsistency which matter. Yet it is true that, in Donne, Woman is rarely allowed to speak for herself and in that respect one may justly have more time for the Thomas Dekker and Thomas Middleton of *The Roaring Girl*.

VI POEMS AND GOD

Donne's religious poetry, substantially the product of the years leading up to ordination, can be seen as a rite of passage between his commitment to a secular career and his decision to be ordained, a decision which led to preferment in the Anglican Church, culminating in the deanship of St Paul's. It will be argued below that the nature of Donne's religious verse fits with this suggestion of a rite of passage, but the point needs to be made, first of all, that this body of verse itself has a rather equivocal existence.

There is nothing inherently surprising about a poet moving, however tentatively, towards ordination producing religious verse. Indeed, it would be more surprising if he did not. Yet Donne showed considerable diffidence about his religious verse and production of it fades out once he is ordained. Such diffidence is itself continuous with his attitudes to his secular poetry, with, that is, the feeling that serious people do not write poetry and that gentlefolk do not publish.[98] At the same time Donne's diffidence about religious verse is not peculiar to him but is consistent with unease in this period about the propriety of religious art. There is perhaps less of a problem for a Catholic, since icons are a comfortable part of the Catholic faith, and there is little sign of diffidence in Bernini or Crashaw. But the puritan revolt against Catholicism raised major questions about religious art and, while it is important to get away from the stereotype of puritan as iconoclast, it is also important not to understate such things as the Vestarian controversy and popular resistance to Laud's 'innovations'.[99] It is also relevant to note that defining a position on religious art may be a particular problem for moderate protestants – and poets. A protestant with Arminian leanings, like Laud himself, will wish to encourage religious art without seeming crypto-Catholic (as Laud tried to do, with little success):[100] hence, perhaps, George Herbert's emphasis upon a sober, clean church decoration and his equivalently restrained, 'pure' poetic style. Obviously, too, a serious religiously-minded poet will not easily turn away from the idea of using his or her talents to serve God, even while such a poet may well think of this idea as perhaps the prompting of the devil and that to cease using the talent might be the poet's most acceptable gift to God. Donne may have even felt that it was improper for a poet who had used religious terminology for 'profane' purposes to then recycle his talents in God's cause.

This continuity of language is one part of what is involved in noticing, as so many critics have done, that Donne's movement from secular to religious involves no abrupt break, but rather a refocusing. There is neither a clean division into secular and religious periods nor a clear stylistic discontinuity. If religious language is now redirected to orthodox religious subjects, that of sexuality is now redeployed to the service of religious experience, most familiarly with:

> Take me to you, imprison me, for I
> Except you enthral me, never shall be free,
> Nor ever chaste, except you ravish me.
> (Divine Meditations 14, ll. 12–14)

and:

> . . . let mine amorous soul court thy mild dove,
> Who is most true, and pleasing to thee, then
> When she' is embraced and open to most men.
> (Divine Meditations 18, ll. 12–14)

In the same way the striking, aggressive openings of secular poems – 'Busy old fool, unruly sun . . .' ('The Sun Rising'), 'for God's sake hold your tongue, and let me love' ('The Canonization') – are repeated in religious poems: 'Spit in my face ye Jews . . .', 'Batter my heart, three-personed God . .' (Divine Meditations 11 and 14). A feeling for wit and paradox continues to be evident, in the riddling of the image of the cross ('The Cross'), in the elaboration of the cosmographic image in 'Hymn to God my God, in my sickness' and, more generally, in the restless pressures put on analogies to see what the signifiers may yield for the signifieds. Here one might compare the way in which the bullet image at the end of 'The Dissolution' seeks to 'prove' that the poet-figure's soul may outstrip that of the dead addressee with the use of legal imagery to encourage conviction that the New Testament's dispensation applies to the poet-figure (Divine Meditations 13).

There are other continuities as well. The emphasis upon first-person pronouns continues, sixteen of these dominating 'Thou hast made me . . .' (Divine Meditations 1) and emerging strongly at the end of 'Good Friday, 1613. Riding Westward':

> O think me worth thine anger, punish me,
> Burn off my rusts, and my deformity,
> Restore thine image, so much, by thy grace,
> That thou mayst know me, and I'll turn my face.

Equally striking is the opening of 'Hymn to God my God, in my sickness':

> Since I am coming to that holy room,
>   Where, with thy choir of saints for evermore,
> I shall be made thy music; as I come
>   I tune the instrument here at the door,
> And what I must do then, think here before.

These examples show not only a prominence of first-person pronouns but also the same vivid imagining of self-in-situation that we find, for example, at the end of 'On his Mistress' (Elegy 16) or in 'The Damp':

> When I am dead, and doctors know not why,
>   And my friends' curiosity
> Will have me cut up to survey each part . . .
>   (ll. 1–3)

Moreover, the restless, shifting moods of the secular poems are matched in the religious and, in particular, the extreme grief and melancholy of such poems as 'Twicknam Garden' and 'A nocturnal upon St Lucy's Day' find their counterparts in the 'low, devout melancholy' which runs through the *La Corona* sonnets and, as 'Dead clods of sadness' ('A Litany' l. 128), becomes such an important part of the Divine Mediations, in which the apostasy of despair often seems very close:

> Yet grace, if thou repent, thou canst not lack;
> But who shall give thee that grace to begin?
>   (Divine Meditations 4, ll. 9–10)

> . . . black sin hath betrayed to endless night
> My world's both parts, and, oh, both parts must die.
>   (Divine Meditations 5, ll. 3–4)

Yet it would be seriously misleading to suggest that Donne's religious poems are finally similar to any of the more famous examples of his secular verse. In satires, erotic elegies and lyrics, as we have seen, the usual postures of the personae are aggressive and assimilative – 'She' is all states, and all princes, I' ('The Sun Rising', l. 21); 'Nature's lay idiot, I taught thee to love' (Elegy 7, l. 1). The voices are characteristically assertive, controlling, commanding:

> Away thou fondling motley humourist,
> (Satire I, l. 1)

> I'll tell thee now (dear love) what thou shalt do . . .
> ('A Valediction: of the Book', l. 1)

> Love, any devil else but you,
> Would for a given soul give something too.
> ('Love's Exchange', ll. 1–2)

In the religious poems, however, although the same prominent sense of self is found, the postures have changed. Supplication is more common than assertion:

> . . . let their flames retire,
> And burn me O Lord . . .
> (Divine Meditations 5, ll. 12–13)

> Impute me righteous . . .
> (Divine Meditations 6, l. 13)

> Teach me how to repent . . .
> (Divine Meditations 7, l. 13)

And poems often open with conditional phrasing:

> If faithful souls be alike glorified . . .
> (Divine Meditations 8, l. 1)

> If poisonous minerals, and if that tree . . .
> (Divine Meditations 9, l. 1)

> Let man's soul be a sphere . . .
> ('Good Friday, 1613 . . .', l. 1)

or with questioning:

> Wilt thou forgive that sin where I begun,
>   Which was my sin, though it were done before?
>   ('A Hymn to God the Father', ll. 1–2)
>
> Thou hast made me, and shall thy work decay?
>   (Divine Meditations 1, l. 1)

Moreover, the postures of these poet-figures are commonly attempts at submission (the figuring of God as adamant to 'draw mine iron heart', Divine Mediations 1, l. 14) or at a reduction of self through battering or quenching, both images occurring together in *La Corona* 7 ('Ascension'):

> O strong ram, which hast battered heaven for me,
> Mild lamb, which with thy blood, hast marked the path;
> . . .
> Oh, with thine own blood quench thine own just wrath . . .
>   (ll. 9–10, 12)

The poet-figures which so consistently demand to be remembered in the secular poems now welcome (or claim to welcome) oblivion:

> That thou remember them, some claim as debt,
> I think it mercy, if thou wilt forget.
>   (Divine Meditations 9, ll. 13–14)

'I have a sin of fear' says the poet-figure of 'A Hymn to God the Father' (l. 13), and it seems no exaggeration. Instead of controlling, these poet-figures ask to be controlled, to be battered, burnt or ravished into submission; and they consistently, anxiously, seek assurance that contracts will be kept – 'oh let that last will stand!' (Divine Meditations 16, l. 14); 'But swear by thy self . . .' ('A Hymn to God the Father', l. 15). God has the power to fulfil a contract, swear an oath, act as 'kind husband' (Divine Meditations 18, l. 11), to be jealous ('A Hymn to Christ . . .'). In terms of the roles defined in the erotic poetry, the poet-figures of the religious poems are scarcely recognisable, until we notice that now they adopt the postures commonly defined for the 'girls' of the erotic verse – and here, of course, the clearest signal is the recurrent appeal to ravishment – this male poet, so often figuring sexual love in terms of coercion and aggression, comes, through his 'sin of fear', to adopt the role wishfully attributed to the female.

But the images of violence – battering, burning, ravishment – may also remind us of the disembowelling knife of the Lincoln's Inn epithalamion, and there is indeed an interesting link between the poet-figures of Donne's religious verse and those of his epithalamia, verse letters and funereal elegies. In such poems the poet-figures are often self-consciously inferior, asserting the greatness of the addressees, 'studying' the models they provide, offering self as something 'refined' by them, being 'recorder' or 'prophet' ('Madam, Reason is our soul's left hand', 'Madam, You have refined me', 'Madam, Man to God's image'). The stances reflect the realities both of Donne's situation after marriage and before ordination and of the whole world of Jacobean patronage. The results, of course, include the need to idealise Elizabeth Drury and eulogise the sordid Somerset–Essex marriage. The postures of the poet-figures are similar to those of the religious poems, although projected with less violence and less emphasis. God becomes the patron: if Bedford was deified in verse letters, her power to refine the poet-figure has passed into God's hands. Also, the suggestion that God becomes patron (with all the implications of power, control, paternal authority) operates on two levels. In the first place, it helps to define the poet's spiritual need to redefine self in terms of trusting submission before there can be any confidence in salvation, any spiritual comfort. In the second it can be related to something more material – to the poet's movement from a search for secular patronage to that of the Anglican Church, whose great figures controlled so many of the livings, so much preferment. Another way of putting this would be to see Donne's transition as being from appeals to the power of James I (as head of state) to appeals to his power as religious patron (as head of church). James, of course, consistently refused to offer Donne secular preferment but as consistently showed willingness to offer religious advancement.

Yet although the roles of the poet-figures are so different in the religious poems from those in the erotic verse, while being interestingly similar to those in the poems to patrons, it remains true that these roles are not only defined stylistically in terms familiar from the erotic poems but also that the change of roles can be seen as masking a continuity which goes beyond style. It has been suggested earlier that the aggressive confidence of satires, erotic elegies and secular lyrics is itself uncertain, exposing itself through the restlessness of style and posture. The poet-figure of Satire I, for example, is persecuted by the 'fondling motley humourist' even while self-consciously asserting his superiority to his tormentor. In the satires, Court fascinates even while it repels, while in the erotic elegies love exists in a world of uncertainty and betrayal; in the *Songs and Sonets* one mood quickly gives way to another and love is seen as an achievement hard to reach, when worth reaching, and never to be relaxed with. Death, infidelity, a change of mind, a new image or cadence may alter things at any moment.

What happens in the religious poems is not that such uncertainty passes but that the strategies for dealing with it change. Fear, a sense of denial, depression, insecurity become more prominent, more obvious in the religious poems, but they are scarcely new themes for Donne. Some connections are fairly evident, as with the moods of 'Twicknam Garden' and 'Nocturnal . . .' and with the bitterness of 'Community' and 'The Apparition', but there is a more general and more significant similarity in what is best described as a lack of trust or 'sin of fear'. The confident assertions of the erotic poems are undercut by the shifting brilliance of the style, as by the sheer variety of mood and assertion. In the religious poems control is given up to God and a narrower range of moods is articulated, but no greater assurance follows. The style of the erotic poems seeks to define Woman and erotic love, while seeming always to admit that both defy settled definition. In the religious poems control is formally handed to God, but here the style seeks to catch another ineffable with as little success. Neither the God of eros or the God of agape seems consistently trustworthy, and this is so because the poet-figures cannot consistently trust anything, try as they may.

The closing lines of 'Good Friday, 1613 . . .' epitomise a great deal of the view of God found in Donne's religious verse:

> O Saviour, as thou hang'st upon the tree;
> I turn my back to thee, but to receive
> Corrections, till thy mercies bid thee leave.
> O think me worth thine anger, punish me,
> Burn off my rusts, and my deformity,
> Restore thine image, so much, by thy grace,
> That thou mayst know me, and I'll turn my face.

The movement to apostasy ('I turn my back') is checked ('but to receive/Corrections') but the poet-figure needs chastising and God is the chastiser, whipping and burning so that the speaker may be assured of his worth and able to turn again to God.

The sense of doubt and of the worthlessness of self is strong in these poems, and with this comes the agony of spiritual dryness:

> Moist, with one drop of thy blood, my dry soul.
> (*La Corona* 5, l. 14)

Doubt about self is proper in a Christian but its danger lies in the temptation to doubt God; passivity may be proper humility but is not a great distance from inertia and despair. A sense of God's mercy thus becomes vital and Donne's most striking articulation of this awareness is found in Divine Meditations 13:

> Tears in his eyes quench the amazing light,
> Blood fills his frowns, which from his pierced head fell,
> And can that tongue adjudge thee unto hell,
> Which prayed forgiveness for his foes' fierce spite?
> No, no . . .
>
> (ll. 5–9)

The poem goes on, by way of 'but as . . . so I say to thee', to argue by analogy with a neo-Platonic account of beauty in 'profane mistresses' that mercy will operate because 'This beauteous form assures a piteous mind'. Damnation, however, *is* part of Christ's function (as the harrowing of hell demonstrates) and so the emphasis falls on 'thee' – unless Donne is anticipating later seventeenth-century views about the salvation of everyone.[101] The negatives which open the sestet are clearly meant as reassurances, but for a moment look like Faustus' last attempts to deny his own damnation, and the working out of the neo-Platonic analogy is typically indirect and conditional. Just how tense all this is can be seen if one compares Donne's poem with George Herbert's 'Love III'.

Faustus came to plead for his own annihilation at the end of Marlowe's play and Donne's poet-figures come close to such a plea ('I think it mercy if thou wilt forget'). The pervasive imagery of burning, whipping and drowning is, of course, corrective but it comes close to destruction, the sense of worthlessness, of being a fit subject for punishment, being relentlessly spelt out as the first three stanzas of 'A Litany' examine the Trinity. The Father is asked to 're-create me, now grown ruinous' by 'purging' 'All vicious tinctures'; the poet-figure's heart is to be drowned in the blood of the crucified Son; and the 'Half wasted' poet-temple 'Must with new storms be weatherbeat' by the Holy Spirit.

Alan Sinfield[102] has emphasised the strength of Calvinism in Donne, and is surely right to do so. The Calvinist stress upon the depravity of humankind is powerfully voiced in Donne's religious verse and pure Calvinism makes passivity seem inevitable. But an emphasis upon Donne's Calvinism (and indeed upon the strength of Calvinism in Elizabethan and Stuart writing, about which Sinfield writes so persuasively) needs to be contextualised, particularly with a writer who began in Catholicism. Calvin himself began there and John Bossy has reminded us that Calvin's account of human depravity is not, of itself, un-Catholic.[103] It would therefore be a mistake to see Donne as wrenching himself from Catholicism merely by projecting this sense of unworthiness. Secondly, Patrick Collinson has made the point that Anglicanism was strongly Calvinist even at the top of the early seventeenth-century church,[104] Arminianism being a reaction against this which begins to make headway after 1610. Donne's Calvinism does not isolate him from main-line Anglicanism.

The evidence of Donne's religious verse is not of doctrinal purity, if by that we mean Protestant rigour. The emphasis on depravity and the importance of divine mercy, together with the absence of any stress on 'works', is orthodox Calvinism, but no concern is shown with Vestarian issues or with images (and this again aligns Donne with the relatively latitudinarian protestantism at the top of the Anglican Church in the early seventeenth century). 'The Cross' is made up by finding images of the crucifixion in nature and its opening reads almost as a critique of iconoclasm:

> Since Christ embraced the Cross itself, dare I
> His image, th' image of his Cross deny?
> Would I have profit by the sacrifice,
> And dare the chosen altar to despise?

Here one is reminded that Puritan concern with icons extended to the placing and naming of altars, about which there was to be trouble in the time of Laudian power.[105] Donne, moreover, can find a prominent place at times in his theology for the Virgin Mary, 'that fair blessed mother maid,/Whose flesh redeemed us; that she-cherubin,/Which unlocked Paradise . . .' ('A Litany', ll. 37–9) although it is interesting that his religious poems give less prominence to the Virgin as a mediating figure than we find with the pseudo-Virgins of poems like the 'Anniversaries'.

If one accepts the view that the Anglicanism of the early seventeenth century is hybrid Calvinism, with a fundamentally Calvinist theology co-existing with residual Catholicism, there seems to be no reason to deny that Donne's religious verse is orthodox Anglicanism of its time. It may then be contrasted with George Herbert's restrained Arminianism and with the seemingly quite relaxed Anglican protestantism of Quarles, Breton and Wither. This is not to deny that a poet like Donne would have done well to avoid giving any grounds for accusations of crypto-Catholicism: the Gunpowder Plot of 1605 and Papist fears of 1610 helped to keep English phobia about Rome alive, and Laudians were to learn how dangerous it could be to steer protestantism too close to Catholicism. We should expect Donne, with the strong Catholic context discussed earlier, to be sensitive to this, particularly as he comes closer to Anglican orders. But it is also worth remembering that anyone with an eye to preferment in the Anglican Church would also do well to avoid the other extreme – any position that might hint at separatist tendencies.[106] The 1606 Act of Allegiance was, after all, designed to draw Catholics into the established church and symbolised the Anglican establishment's desire (as much political as doctrinal) to be able to include as many English as possible. Among these there may have been many who felt the reality of the questions of Divine Meditations 18:

> Show me dear Christ, thy spouse, so bright and clear.
> What, is it she, which on the other shore
> Goes richly painted? or which robed and tore
> Laments and mourns in Germany and here?
>
> (ll. 1–4)

Anglicanism, it might be suggested, was trying to show that it embraced most answers to such questions.

The claim that Donne's religious verse is orthodox in terms of early seventeenth-century Anglicanism is not meant to sound reductive. The urgency and the vividness of the best poems stamp them as characteristically Donne, and the urgent tensions of the writing can obviously be related to the particular circumstances of Donne's birth and life. Yet, when we remember how many English men and women had similar choices to make, it seems proper to put less weight upon the idiosyncracy of Donne's verse than upon it as a remarkably striking version of an Anglican position which, at least in a public sense, is that of a majority.

It is conventional enough to draw a distinction between those of Donne's religious poems which seem urgent in their nervous movement, compressed syntax and violent verbal listings and those (like the *La Corona* sonnets) which read more like attempts to versify conventional religious positions or ceremonies. Such a distinction is useful in establishing where Donne is most alive as a poet, and few would deny that this is when his 'sin of fear' is most active and most fiercely focused upon versions of self. But I think that the dichotomy is in another sense misleading and that terms like 'urgent' and 'forced' apply to both, albeit in different ways.

The urgency which fear and doubt give especially to a number of the Divine Meditations is something which finally reduces the chances that the poems will seem to answer their own doubts at other than a rhetorical level. The answers to Donne's doubts lie in faith – faith in the possibility of divine mercy and in God's power over Satan and death. For a Christian to know this, however, is nothing unless it is also felt, experienced, believed, although belief in the knowledge may keep despair at bay while the soul is dry. Donne's religious poems know where they are going, do not conclude in heresy or apostasy, but the poetic pressure is articulated with a rhetoric which foregrounds doubt and fear to the extent that the rhetoric is itself the peril, making despair almost seductive. So the powerful belittlement of death in Divine Meditations 10 ('Death be not proud . . .') betrays fear and a weakness of argument which undercut the expressed conclusion. The sharpness and energy of the imaginings of the end of the world in 'At the round earth's imagined corners . . .' (Divine Meditations 7) and of the poet-figure as surrogate Christ in 'Spit in my face ye Jews . . .' (Divine Meditations 11) are such as to push the poems close to heresy. This allows it to be argued that Donne's finest religious poems are temptations to despair precisely because they are

artistic forcings of impulses conducive to despair – a strong sense
of worthlessness, an inability to realise a sense of divine mercy.
Clearly, in so far as the poems became public when published,
this expression of temptation itself could be dangerous for any
committed but uncertain believer. Paradoxically, what checks the
tendency to despair is the stubbornness of the ego, the fascination
shown with 'I' figures even as the lines ask for that 'I' to be
whipped or burnt or drowned. A development of this point
would be to say that it is the ability of the poems to complete
themselves formally which checks the impulse to disintegration
or even annihilation (rather as it is the ability formally to complete
King Lear which prevents that play from being finally totally
pessimistic).

The same line of argument allows us to see those poems, like
the *La Corona* sonnets, which lack the sense of urgency of the
greatest religious lyrics, as urgent in another way. Here the word
play seems automatic and external:

> . . . thou art now
> Thy Maker's maker, and thy Father's mother,
> Thou hast light in dark; and shutt'st in little room,
> Immensity cloistered in thy dear womb.
> (*La Corona* 2, 'Annunciation' ll. 11–14)

In 'A Litany' a lack of imaginative inwardness emerges in rhythmical deadness:

> And thy illustrious zodiac
> Of twelve apostles, which engirt this all,
> (From whom whosoever do not take
> Their light, to dark deep pits, throw down, and fall,)
> (ll. 73–6)

In both cases Donne is writing to a predetermined pattern and
these patterns are ones outside the poet. It can be suggested that
Donne is never most alive when working in this way, but it can
also be argued that, being no Antinomian, salvation can only
come for him if the poet-figures can articulate a convincing
shaping of self within positions not invented by that self. God
makes the patterns, not the poet. The failures to write convincingly
in *La Corona* and 'A Litany' mark the urgency of the need to do so.

In that sense these less convincing poems are important parts of the whole picture.

Queen Elizabeth is famously reported as having wished to avoid letting windows upon the souls of her subjects,[107] but the religious struggles of the sixteenth and seventeenth centuries are such as to make this seem only one part of a sentence, the rest of which would run something like 'but it is often necessary to do so'. Ultimately the windows are necessary because of the identification of church and state, whereby it is almost impossible to conceive of dissent from the established church as other than dangerous to both church and state. English Catholics tried in vain to have a division accepted, by which their loyalty to the state and monarch would not be seen as undermined by their adherence to Rome. In the middle of the seventeenth century sectarians tried to establish that passivism and separatism need not be seditious. Both failed. One consequence of this linking of state and church is that there is a point at which religious faith cannot be seen as a purely private matter. A degree of toleration could be manifest (partly because the imposition of uniformity was so difficult) but never secure. In this sense it is misleading to think of Donne's religious concerns as purely private or to imagine him thinking they were so. Salvation is a matter of accommodating self to something beyond self: Calvinism is congregational and separatism remains a matter of 'gatherings' even if those gathered are very few. The solo possibilities of Antinomianism are well beyond Donne's reach.

This is not to deny the importance of searching the individual soul, but the point of this remains the identification of that soul with others in a church of some sort. The final stage of Donne's life, of course, sees him ordained into a church and gaining fame and preferment as priest and dean within Jacobean Anglicanism.

3
1615–1632

I BIOGRAPHICAL OUTLINE

When John Donne was ordained deacon and priest in January 1615, he adopted perhaps his most clearly defined role and began the most public phase of his life. Role-playing had been strong in Donne as far back as we can trace his life in any detail, and he seems always to have been aware of an audience, but the short period as one of Egerton's secretaries was, in our terms, the only time before 1615 when Donne was in full-time employment, if we exclude short engagements with such as Drury. Moreover, the role of priest defined a public function of preaching, taking services and living to a high standard of expected behaviour, while ordination into the Anglican Church also meant a formal statement of adherence to its doctrines. Thus the role is one which Donne chose to adopt, rather than one he had shaped for himself.

Izaak Walton stresses the break which the ordination represents. He gives King James a major part to play, as one who 'gave a positive denial to all requests' for secular advancement for Donne but who is also represented as saying:

> I know Mr Donne is a learned man, has the abilities of a learned Divine; and will prove a powerful Preacher, and my desire is to prefer him that way, and in that way, I will deny you nothing for him.[1]

Walton records Donne's delay in taking orders, turning this to Donne's credit and emphasising the idea of conversion:

> Now the English Church had gain'd a second St. Austine, for, I think, none was so like him before his Conversion: none so like St. Ambrose after it: and if his youth had the infirmities of the one, his age had the excellencies of the other; the learning and holiness of both.[2]

101

By this account Donne moves, by way of conversion, from youth to age; and in a letter to Sir Edward Herbert he himself refers to his ordination as involving 'such a change, as, if my unworthynes did not avile it, were an addition': he has 'by the orders of our churche, receyved a new character'.[3] Both Walton and Donne are dramatising, but they are recording a decisive moment in the latter's life.

James, according to Walton, said that he would deny Donne nothing once he had been ordained, and signs of favour were quickly shown, though not all of these are directly attributable to the king. Donne became rector of Keyston and Sevenoaks in January and July 1616 respectively and Reader in Divinity at Lincoln's Inn in October. Royal favour was more directly shown in Donne's appointment as a royal chaplain very soon after ordination and in the granting of the degree of Doctor of Divinity to him by the University of Cambridge in March 1615. Walton mentions this, but gives a carefully neutral account, whereby James 'was pleased to recommend (Donne) to the University' and the Vice-Chancellor, knowing Donne as 'Author of that learned Book the Pseudo-Martyr ... proposed it to the University, who presently assented, and exprest a gladness, that they had such an occasion to intitle him to be theirs'.[4] Bald, however, offers evidence of a reluctant university yielding to pressure from the king.[5] In April 1616 Donne preached at Court for the first time, another indication of royal favour.

Very soon after ordination, in fact, the main lines of Donne's ministry were established – the duties of a rector (which Donne seems to have taken seriously)[6] and a preaching circuit which took in his rectories but which also included both the Inns of Court and the king's court as well as the great public event of preaching at Paul's Cross, where Donne appeared for the first time in March 1617. Preaching and the other duties of clerical office (the latter more marked after Donne became Dean of St Paul's in November 1621) continue to be the staple of the last period of his life: Donne died in office, preaching almost to the end. But the secular dimensions of his life do not simply disappear.

Donne was about sixty years old when he died, well above average for the seventeenth century,[7] and a feature of the last quarter of his life is the loss of family and friends. His wife died in 1617. She gave birth to a still-born child on 10 August and died on the 15th, at the age of 33, 'worn out by child-bearing while still scarcely past her youth'.[8] She had been, Bald reminds us, twelve times in child-bed and seven children survived her. Such evidence of her married life as survives suggests that it cannot have been easy, even if one accepts that Donne was a devoted husband to her. Making the point that 'The personality of (Donne's) wife inevitably remains elusive', Bald goes on to speak of her mainly as a compensation to Donne 'for his mercurial temperament'.[9] One would like to know how the marriage looked from Ann's perspective. Both Walton and Bald may be felt to present Donne's grief at his wife's death rather uncritically, but there is no reason to doubt that Donne did grieve or that he looked after the surviving children conscientiously.

In 1627 Lady Bedford and Lady Danvers (Magdalen Herbert) both died, while in 1628 Christopher Brooke died and Buckingham was assassinated by Felton. Donne thus lost one of his oldest friends (Brooke), two patrons who were nearly friends (Bedford, Danvers) and, in Buckingham, one of those great men whose potential help had meant so much to Donne before 1615. Donne also outlived his own mother, by about two months. Despite her continued Catholicism she had been living with Donne towards the end of her life[10] and his letter to her 'after the death of her Daughter', perhaps of 1616, is an interesting indication not only of love and respect but of how genuine Donne's ecumenicism was.[11]

These deaths break various strands between Donne and his past, and must also have encouraged that contemplation of death which seems almost inevitable in a society in which mortality presses so heavily and which seems so natural to Donne.[12] But other features of Donne's life after 1615 continue to remind us of earlier ambitions. In 1622 he became a JP in Kent and Bedford and was still a Bedford magistrate in 1626–30. He was involved at various times in the clerical courts,[13] became an honorary member of the Virginia Company in 1622, and had a painful dispute with his son-in-law, Edward Alleyn, the former actor, in 1625. The favour of James meant that, for the first time in his life, he was genuinely accepted at Court, able to think seriously of promotion to a bishopric,[14] while as Dean of St Paul's he had power and responsibility beyond anything he had previously experienced. Meanwhile, however, illnesses in 1623, 1625 and 1630 provided a rather different kind of continuity with the past (although the significance of this should not be over-stressed, given the low general level of Jacobean health and Donne's qualities of self-dramatisation).

There is good reason to see the last period of Donne's life as its most satisfying. It is striking how active he was (one of Bald's chapters is called 'Active Years') and it is tempting to contrast this with the images of entrapment between 1601 and 1615. The surviving letters from this last period are calmer, less introspective than earlier ones. Even if Walton seems concerned to exaggerate the 'conversion' symbolised by ordination, and even if one notices the tentativeness of the poem 'To Mr Tilman after he had taken orders' there does seem to be a case for regarding the future Dr Donne as a man who had found himself and who was able to function efficiently and confidently, despite illnesses, the problems of looking after children as a single parent, and the shocks of the deaths of friends, relatives and patrons.

The rest of this chapter will look more closely at certain features of this last period of Donne's life, at his role as preacher, his doctrinal position, the literary product, and at Donne's death.

II DONNE AND PREACHING

In a letter to George Gerrard, not many months before his death, Donne takes vehement exception to rumours that he has not really been ill but has pretended illness 'to save charges, and to live at ease, discharged of preaching'. On the contrary, Donne tells Gerrard, 'It hath been my desire . . . that I might die in the Pulpit; . . . that is, die the sooner by occasion of my former labours'.[15] Walton's account of Donne as a preacher suggests that his preaching was of such quality that death in the pulpit could have been seen as an apotheosis:

> A Preacher in earnest; weeping sometimes for his Auditory, sometimes with them: always preaching to himself, like an Angel from a cloud, but in none; carrying some, as St. Paul was, to Heaven in holy raptures, and inticing others by a sacred Art and Courtship to amend their lives; here picturing a vice so as to make it ugly to those that practised it; and a vertue so, as to make it be beloved even by those that lov'd it not; and all this with a most particular grace and an unexpressible addition of comeliness.[16]

Donne was a proud man, very much aware of social status; priesthood was not a socially dignified profession in the early seventeenth century;[17] an emphasis upon the preaching function is one mark of a protestant stress rather than a Catholic one. Donne dwells upon the dignity of the preacher, thus transforming the priesthood itself. So, at the opening of a sermon 'Preached to the King, at White-Hall, the first of April, 1627', Donne presents Christ himself as a preacher, speculating about his methodology, wondering if the text in Mark's gospel (4:24) from which his own text is taken 'be one intire Sermon of our Saviours, preached at once, or Notes taken and erected from severall Sermons of his . . .'. Christ as preacher entrusts 'the Mystery of salvation' to his apostles, who are to 'publish' this 'by their Preaching, their Ministery, their Apostleship' (*Sermons*, VII.16.393–4). Since 'Preaching is Gods ordinance . . . to beget Faith, to take away preaching, were to disarme God' (IV.7.192, 195): a preacher is thus part of God's armament and is heir, via the apostles, to Christ's own role.

When Donne expatiates upon how the preacher operates 'to beget faith' we find imagery familiar to any reader of the religious poems:

God's Ordinance of preaching batters the soule, and by that breach, the Spirit enters; His Ministers are an Earth-quake, and shake an earthly soule; They are the sonnes of thunder, and scatter a cloudy conscience; They are as the fall of waters, and carry with them whole Congregations: 3000 at a Sermon, 5000 at a Sermon, a whole City, such a City as Niniveh at a Sermon; and they are as the roaring of a Lion, where the Lion of the tribe of Juda, cries down the Lion that seekes whom he may devour; that is, Orthodoxall and fundamentall truths, are established against clamorous and vociferant innovations. (VII.16.396)

The pun on 'Ordinance' brings in the imagery of battering and drowning. Ministers as earthquakes act the role of deity. The prose relishes the power,[18] but the power is at the service of orthodoxy against 'innovation'. As preacher Donne achieves the status for which he had been looking for many years; becomes a kind of monarch, almost a god.

The last lines of this quotation indicate Donne's care to anchor his high estimate of the preacher's role in the concept of service to the English church and state. Part of the preacher's function consists of a 'fixt and constant course of conteining Subjects in their Religious and Civill duties . . .' (IV.7.194). But Donne is also careful to define the preacher's role in such a way as to fix it in Jacobean Anglicanism. The Christ-derived role of preacher, with its responsibility for begetting faith by explicating scripture, is not prominent, Donne claims, in Catholicism, even though 'it be true, that the Reformation . . . have so much prevailed upon them, as that they have now twenty Sermons in that Church, for one that they had before Luther' (VII.16.401). Preaching is thus a Protestant glory, but if Donne is anxious to distance himself from Catholicism in this respect he is also concerned to create equivalent distance from protestant extremism. This is done by stressing the need for the preacher to be learned, for 'Can any man hope to make a good Preacher, as soone as a good Picture? In three or foure dayes, or with three or foure Books?' (IV.7.202). Later in the same sermon this is spelt out: 'Those Preachers which must save your soules, are not ignorant, unlearned extemporall men . . .' (IV.7.209). Donne commits himself firmly to the Anglican cause of a learned preaching ministry[19] and sets himself clearly against both Catholic neglect of the preaching function and 'puritan' encouragment of a democratic ministry which might admit tradesmen and even women.[20]

One of the two sermons I have been quoting from was preached from Paul's Cross in September 1622 and this sermon, according to Bald,[21] was consciously shaped to serve King James. In the context, on the one hand, of the king's seeming softness to Catholics in the delicate circumstances of the negotiations for Charles to marry a Spanish bride and, on the other, of the dangers to European Protestantism, James tried to calm national unease by issuing his 'Directions to Preachers' on 4 August 1622. These acknowledge the social and political importance of preaching by forbidding all preachers to 'meddle with matters of state' and severely restricting pulpit discussions of 'deep points' of doctrine.[22] In his sermon Donne acts as interpreter of the Directions, thus associating himself very firmly with king, Court and State Anglicanism: 'It is the Head of the Church that declares to us those things whereby we are to be ordered' (IV.7.199). The king is presented as the voice of the middle way, desiring a learned priesthood and seeing the Reformation as the means by which 'Papistry was driven out, and Puritanisme kept out, and wee delivered from the Superstition of the Papist, and the madnesse of the Anabaptists' (IV.7.202). This is consistent with the position assumed by Donne in verse,[23] but here Donne is voicing this position as spokesperson for monarch and state: he has a socio-religious role to replace the isolation of the years between marriage and ordination.

The phrase 'God the Father' has a resonance in the seventeenth century which has now largely passed. Despite evidence of a growing tendency to see marriage and parenthood in terms of partnership,[24] the commonplace still, in the early seventeenth century, invests authority in the husband/father. The wife/mother is legally subordinate to him; inheritance is patrilinear; the father is to rule and control. His role is that of the head, as locus of Reason, in relation to the body, where Will and Passion inhere.[25] The monarch (who should ideally be male) is commonly seen as Head and Father. James I was fond of the image and very much concerned to define and develop the theory of Divine Right, whereby the king is appointed by God, who is to be seen as the ultimate King, Head, Father. As these terms interact they draw upon each other and their manifestations in the contexts of Heaven, State and Family, gaining weight and authority from each other.

Each of these types of paternity, headship and monarchy depends upon the presence of something subordinate, something to be ruled and guided: a father's wife, children and servants; the body; subjects. It is not difficult to see how the priest might fit this pattern, with his role being to rule and guide his congregation, and the conventional figuring of priest as shepherd (utilising a pun on 'pastor') is of this same type, the congregation being the flock of sheep.[26] When, as in Jacobean England, there is a state church, the priest of that church participates in the simultaneous duality of the monarch's role, as can be clearly seen, for example, in the Elizabethan Homilies, which, in part, use the pulpit to convey political messages.

If we think specifically of the priest as preacher, however, we can go a step farther. The authoritative centrality or headship of the monarch is ritually represented on state and festive occasions by such objects symbols as the throne in Parliament, the focal seat for Elizabeth in the layout of the court for the trial of Mary of Scots,[27] and in the place for the monarch at masques and plays. Such devices figure the centrality of the monarch and, as that centrality becomes linked with heliocentric thought, the image of monarch as sun strengthens the focal idea:[28] this is the point to which everything comes and from which everything flows. Milton, of course, was to develop the concept of God as king–father–sun into the luminosities of the third book of *Paradise Lost*, and the picture of the monarch centrally seated at trial, masque or in parliament can easily be linked with the centrality of the father in family portraits or at the head of the domestic dining table. All of this, moreover, fits in well with the preacher and with the role of priest as guide (leading his flock, celebrating communion). But the most relevant point of contact here is that the priest-as-preacher faces his congregation and is set apart from it, just as the monarch judicially confronts the object of a state trial or the performers of a play or masque. But in such roles the monarch is simultaneously set apart from and backed by the audience, so that – be it in law court, parliament or theatre – the monarch is both distinct authority and the voice of the audience. The priest as celebrant is the voice of the congregation; as preacher within a state church he is the voice of that church, speaking for it to the congregation–audience, drawing his authority from the state church and seeking to impose that authority upon the congregation. This is very clearly what Donne tries to do in his sermon from St Paul's Cross in 1622. It is the power of the role which makes the preacher dangerous if he is deviant, if, that is, he insists on speaking for himself or for a sect rather than for state and state church.

It is not difficult, in the light of what has been said about Donne's life and career before ordination, to see why the role of priest (especially as preacher) might appeal, or why priesthood with the state church might appeal particularly. The priesthood might lack prestige in a general sense, but the role could be redefined (as Donne does redefine it) and it offered a clear route to advancement, with expansion of the authority already present in the basic role of parish priest. Moreover, the very lack of social prestige could work to Donne's advantage for this reduced problems of entry: no social rite of passage was required. Walton's argument of gentrification by talent at the opening of his 'Life of Donne' fits in well here: genteel status is not essential for entrance to the priesthood or even for advancement in the profession. As preacher, to make an obvious enough point, Donne could assume the authority spoken of above, with the assurance that he had the literary talents to be an effective one. As preacher

Donne finally achieves the power he had been seeking for a long while.

But Donne was scarcely ever an ordinary priest or preacher. Having got virtually nowhere between marriage and ordination, favour comes to him almost simultaneously with ordination. A man who is almost immediately appointed a royal chaplain, who preaches at Court within fifteen months of ordination and who becomes Divinity Reader at Lincoln's Inn in under two years of that event is scarcely a routine ordinand. In 1621 Donne becomes Dean of St Paul's and is soon spoken of as a future bishop.[29] As dean he has a role within the legal system (appointed a judge in the Court of Delegates in 1622) and as a spin-off from his various rectorships he acts as a Justice of the Peace in Kent and Bedford.

In a variety of ways, then, Donne's career in the Anglican Church fulfils, at least on the surface, ambitions which can be discerned long before 1615. As priest and preacher he can be a guide and commander: he can lead and rule congregations and his literary talents can be used to control large audiences from a dominant position, as distinct from seeking to overwhelm single subjects in a love-lyric or to placate/flatter superiors in epistles and epithalamia. Becoming a favoured preacher means opportunities to perform at Court and other prestigious (if sometimes precarious) locations. Becoming dean expands his area of authority, as do the judicial functions which come Donne's way after 1615. Further, Donne, who for so long had been a seeker after patronage, becomes a dispenser of it, a man to whom others turn for places. All of this means that the achievement of gentry status by 1601 can at last be actualised and lived.

The above paragraph needs, however to be qualified. There are still important constraints upon Donne and these are built into the chosen role. Preferment depends upon Donne fitting the specific function of priest in the state church. He is required to be orthodox and this means continuing to accept a subordinate position. A priest (or even a dean) within a state church may have authority dignified by metaphors of headship and fatherhood but remains primarily the spokesperson for the actual head/father of the state and its church and for the God who is the ultimate authority as defined by this state and church. In slightly more concrete terms, this means that success continues to involve being seen to be a convincing servant and a recipient of patronage even while also a dispenser of it. Being close to the king and other great figures meant enhanced possibilities of privilege, but equally this called for vigilance and careful orthodoxy.

The Donne who smashes his secretaryship with Egerton by his secret marriage, who outrages orthodoxies in the *Songs and Sonets*, who struggles to make talent serve naked interest in the Somerset epithalamion and *Pseudo-Martyr*, and who tries to chasten himself in the Hymns and Divine Mediations, does not seem likely to have found it easy to accept the constraints of his role after 1616, even if the power of that role exceeded anything hitherto available to him. In the imagined world of 'The Sun Rising' the poet-figure was not merely *a* king but 'all princes' and ruled over 'all states'. The 'kingdom' Donne came to rule was at best a vassal state, with an immediate secular-religious overlord (the king) and a further, definitive one (God). Donne, drawn, so his writings suggest, both to be king and slave, is not likely to have found the priestly role an easy one, however attractive it may have been.

III   DOCTRINE

In the 'Sermon Preached at Pauls Crosse' in 1622 Donne seems concerned, as we might expect, to place himself as a firm Anglican. There is the Reformist emphasis on 'the plaine wordes of Scripture', but this is checked by the moderation in exhorting 'the people' 'not presently to fall to gnawing of bones, of Controversies, and unrevealed Mysteries'. The Thirty-Nine Articles are glossed as marking out a distinct position for the Anglican Church. So Articles 22 and 28 are seen as setting themselves 'against the Romish Doctrine of Pardons, of Images, of Invocation' and against transubstantiation. The position is that 'of the Protestant against the Romane Church' (IV.7.205–6), but the remark about controversy in the reading of scripture makes it clear that Donne's position is far from extreme. In 1627 (the year in which Laud and Neile were appointed to the Privy Council) Donne, preaching to the king at Whitehall, is again concerned to distance Anglicanism from 'the Roman distemper' and to argue that:

> . . . nearer to (God), and to the institutions of his Christ, can no Church, no not of the Reformation, be said to have come, then ours does. (VII.16.400, 409)

In his 'first Sermon preached to K. Charles at St. James, 1625' Donne had firmly claimed that 'the Lord Jesus himselfe is the Foundation of this Church':

> All's one; the Instructions of Christ, the Doctrine of Christ, the Word, the Scriptures of Christ, are the Foundations of this House. (VI.12.252–5)

This clear and expected Anglicanism allows Donne, preaching 'At the Consecration of Lincolnes Inne Chapell', to defend Lutherans and Calvinists against Belarmine (IV.15.373*f*). But Bald reminds us[30] that Donne also became concerned, around 1626, to defend 'the Church of England ... against the attacks of Puritans, to whom the High Church policy of Laud, obviously favoured by the King, was a growing provocation'. Bald also remarks on Donne's concern, in 1627, over offending Charles and Laud in a sermon at the Chapel Royal in April. Donne seems to have allowed himself to look 'as if he were deliberately following Abbott's lead and taking sides against the polices of Laud'.[31] Donne's anxiety to clear himself may indicate that he was genuinely pro-Laud in 1627, or he may have been chiefly concerned not to risk losing favour. What does seem clear is that Donne's Anglicanism was moderate enough to cope with the movement in the Jacobean church fom Abbott's Calvinism to Laud's Arminianism. There is no need to see this cynically for, as noted earlier, Donne is consistent in taking the view that there is more than one path to God and in inclining to the position that the state church is where nationals belong. Nothing, it seems, that happened within Anglicanism between Donne's ordination and death put undue pressure on this flexible moderation.

What Donne's position meant emerges in more detail if we look at particular aspects of his doctrinal position. He is satirical in a sermon to the Virginia Company about Roman Catholicism's emphasis on miracles: 'a miraculous drawing of a Tooth, a miraculous cutting of a Corne': 'In truth, their greatest Miracle to me, is, that they find men to beleeve their Miracles ...' (IV.10.278). But he is equally against the tendency in the Reformed churches to reduce the number of church festivals:

> Feastes in generall, Feasts instituted by the Church alone, Feasts in their yearly returne and observation, have their use ... (IV.15.369)

Here again Donne is defining an Anglican *via media*, and he does the same over prayer. The Reformed churches tended to permit, even to encourage, impromptu praying, but it is clear that when Donne speaks of 'a right Prayer' he means a set prayer. Speaking specifically of the Lord's Prayer he comments that 'Some of the old Heretiques of the Primitive Church abridged that Prayer, and some of our later Schismatiques have annihilated, evacuated that Prayer' (VII.10.264). A concern with formal prayer and the support of church festivals both indicate an emphasis upon the church as a controlling and defining institution: the individualism of the radical reformists has no appeal. This concern, moreover, is consistent with the moderate protestant view of scripture. Donne's preacher-priest, as we have seen, is a figure of authority and power, one compatible with the Tudor and Stuart view of the priest as vehicle for the promulgation of state and state church positions. It should be added, however, that although this emphasis emphatically divides Donne from the kind of protestantism which virtually abolishes such a priestly role, it does not divide him from orthodox Calvinism, which places considerable weight upon the authority of the pastor.

The suspicions about the myopic scrutiny of texts are made clear in a sermon preached before the king in February 1625, in which it is emphasised that interpretation must be based on 'Gods whole Booke, and not a fewe mis-understood Sentences out of that Booke'. A reader should not vex his/her soul 'with mistaken sentences, but rely upon the establishment of Gods purpose in the whole booke'. Significantly, Donne illustrates his point with the text which defeated Marlowe's Faustus and was so awful a text for Calvinists. He quotes, 'Stipendium peccati mors est' – but adds 'That which must try thee is the whole Booke, the tenor and purpose, the Scope and intention of God in his Scriptures . . .' (VII.2.87–9). The Calvinist Faustus despairs: the Anglican Calvinism of Donne escapes despair by stressing the 'tenor and purpose' of the whole book. Further salvation means listening to the preachers God has ordained (VII.16.395), and so it is no surprise that Donne distinguishes between 'a Lay Dedication, and an Ecclesiasticall Dedication' (IV.15.370).

But perhaps the most important territory fought over in the splits and controversies of Christianity, at least in the period of and leading up to the Reformation, was that which involves predestination, damnation, the efficacy of works and the mercy of God. At one extreme there was the Calvinist emphasis on human depravity and the predestined damnation of most humans; at the other, the suggestions provided by indulgences and pardons that salvation could be acquired by good works, however mechanical, materialistic and downright cynical these might be. It is obvious enough that, within belief, one's location between these extremes was a matter of great urgency. Marlowe's Faustus knew that much, and so did John Donne. Clearly, it is important, when writing of Donne in this context, to try to assess his temperamental involvement in this vital area, but for the moment our concern is primarily with what position he articulates in his sermons.

This is no easy matter to summarise for Donne refers frequently throughout the sermons to the issue of damnation, but it seems that his chief concern is to argue against an extreme Calvinism. Donne labours to establish a God reluctant to damn. So, in a Whitehall Lent sermon of February 1618/19 he works with a typical image from the music of stringed instruments:

> If we shall say, that Gods first string in this instrument, was Reprobation, that Gods first intention, was, for his glory to damn Man; ... so that he might have some body to damn ... there's no musick in all this, no harmony, no peace in such preaching. (II.7.170)

A communion sermon of the same year on the text 'What man is he that liveth, and shall not see death?' (Psalm 89:48) is concerned to stress that 'God made not death, neither hath he pleasure in the destruction of the living' (II.9.207). And the 'Sermon of Valediction' in April argues that God did not make the 'dark fire' of damnation for us 'but much less did he make us for that fire; that is, make us to damn us' (II.11.240). In the Whitehall sermon of 1625 the argument is much the same. 'Some expositors' – 'and fairely', Donne adds – claim that 'There is no necessitie that any Man, any this or that Man should perish'. 'God begins not at judgement, but at Mercie' and although 'there may be a Divorce, a putting away, out of God's sight and service, in any particular Soule', this is 'not done out of any tyrannicall wantonesse in God ...' (VII.2.74–5). The position is well summed up later in this same sermon:

> there is alwayes roome for Repentance, and Mercie, but his Judgements and Executions are certaine, there is no roome for Presumption nor Collusion. (VII.2.77)

And again:

> ... whensoever thou shalt grow due to him, by a new, and a
> true repentance, hee shall re-assume thee, into his bed, and his
> bosome ... (VII.2.93)

What runs through these quotations is the concern not so much
to deny predestination (which was Jacobean Anglican doctrine) as
to modify any tendency to respond to this doctrine by lapsing
into inertia or despair. Donne's emphasis suggests that God's will
is to save rather than to damn, and the implication is of a
plenitude of the saved rather than the sectarian concept of the
salvation of the few. The difference is perhaps psychological
rather than strictly doctrinal.

This attempt to define a God anxious to save allows Donne to
take a positive, if moderate, view of humankind's role: 'though
God give his glorie to none, his glorie, that is to doe all with
Nothing, yet he gives them their glorie, that doe any thing for
him, or for themselves'. Those who 'proceede in that devotion of
assisting Gods cause' shall 'have a place in the booke of life;
indelibly in the Booke of life ...' (IV.7.186). But the key here lies in
what, in a 1626 funeral sermon, Donne calls 'The largenesse of
Gods goodnesse to us' (VII.10.259). For a powerful passage in that
sermon makes it clear that Donne accepts the depravity of the
race. Works of charity must, he says, be called 'good workes' by
'the world that hath benefit by them' – 'but the man that does
them, and knows the weaknesses of them, knows they are not
good works' (VII.10.265). God, however, of his goodness, 'out of
my Confession of the impuritie of my best actions, shall vouchsafe
to take off his eyes from that impurity, as though there were
none; but no spirituall thing in us, not Faith, not Hope, not
Charitie, have any puritie, any perfection in themselves' (ibid.).

Although *Pseudo-Martyr* and *Ignatius* show that controversy was
something which Donne could enter into with expertise and even
relish, the sermons both claim and act out the case against
controversy. This does not mean that Donne fails to define a
position, but that he does not see the sermon as serving controversy. Since, by definition, controversy is adversarial, Donne both
avoids detailed engagement in it (while being concerned to reject
the pretensions of both extreme puritanism and Catholicism) and
concentrates upon establishing a 'sensible' theology which encour-

ages loyalty to the state church, confidence that salvation is a reasonable possibility, and the belief that the individual can, by co-operating with God's good will, facilitate salvation, however unworthy the individual must see herself or himself as being.

There are two important and interacting contexts for this effort. Donne is clearly trying in his sermons to act out the role of the responsible preacher-priest in the Jacobean and early Caroline church. Having, with ordination and promotion in that church, a clear social role, almost for the first time since his marriage, Donne labours to fulfil expectations. He preaches frequently and he preaches orthodoxy and loyalty, responding sensitively enough to the movement towards Arminianism to remain faithful to that role even as it changes. Secondly, however, there is a more directly personal context. A concern to find a religious role and position antedates Donne's ordination, and may be seen as leading to it. Donne, it feels, was less concerned with niceties of doctrine than with which church he could embrace with sufficient conviction to believe that he could be saved within it. So although the sermons are public statements serving public functions, they may also be seen as debates with self, their function then being to argue for the preacher's own capacity for salvation. It is the interplay of this duality which gives Donne's best sermons their peculiar quality, and so they must, in part, be seen as material and as literature.

IV SERMONS AS PRODUCT

Bald quotes from the conclusion of a letter Donne wrote to Sir Thomas Roe in November 1625:

> I have reviewed as many of my Sermons, as I had kept any notes of; and I have written out, a great many, and hope to do more.[32]

If Bald's earlier account[33] of Donne's practice is correct, and there is no good reason to doubt it, we can usefully distinguish three strands in the preparation of a typical Donne sermon. Firstly (and, as he acknowledges, Bald is following Walton) 'Donne planned his sermons, collected and organised his materials ... he made plentiful notes and may, on occasion, have written out the sermon in full before delivery'. Secondly, however, 'he would have delivered his sermons either with no notes at all or with a minimum of notes'. The third strand would be the writing up of the sermon with an eye on publication, this sometimes being done years later.

If this is indeed the way in which Donne's sermons reached the form in which they survive, we cannot know the exact relationship between the published product and the delivered one; and it also means that we are dealing with literary texts rather than transcriptions of an oral event, although it should be added that the texts read as reconstructions of such events, 'literary memorials'. Moreover, even a literary sermon (like a closet drama) is based upon the idea of delivery – of a preacher and an audience. It is worth adding that, although a sermon audience is presumably plural in reality, a number of Donne's sermons clearly accept the principle that if the monarch is present on such an occasion as the giving of a sermon he or she is the focal, singular audience. The sense of audience (always important in Donne's work) is very strong in the sermons as published. This is partly a matter of the care with which titles re-establish the occasions of particular sermons: 'Preached at S. Dunstanes upon Trinity-Sunday. 1627' (on Revelations 4:8); 'A Sermon of Commemoration of the Lady Danvers . . . Preach'd at Chilsey, where she was lately buried . . . 1 July 1627' (on 2 Peter 3:13); 'Preached to the King at White-hall, upon the occasion of the Fast, April 5, 1628' (on Psalm 6:6,7) (VIII.1,2,8). But there is also the way in which Donne shapes sermon to audience, as with 'To the Honourable the Virginia Company' (IV.10). Beyond this again, structure and style are clearly organised with audience in mind.

A representative example of Donne's most common structural method is 'A Lent-Sermon Preached at White-hall, February 12. 1618' (II.7). The text is Ezekiel 33:32, and it is significant, remembering Donne's comments on texts and 'whole books',[34] that very near the sermon's opening, he contextualises the verse from Ezekiel through quotations from elsewhere in chapter 33. He then goes on to offer preliminary comment on the text:

First then, God for his own glory promises here, that his Prophet, his Minister shall be *Tuba* . . . (p. 166)

This done, the preacher clearly and carefully lays out his sub-divisions:

> These then are our parts that make up this increpation: First, the Prophet shall do his part fully: Secondly, the people shall do some of theirs: But then lastly, they shall fail in the principal, and so make all uneffectual. (p. 168)

The parts are separately developed, utilising other scriptural texts, and then drawn together in conclusion. It is important to notice how careful Donne is to signal where the sermon is and where it is going, as the openings of a run of paragraphs in another sermon make clear:

> But what glory can God receive from man . . . ?
>
> But, as there is a place cited by S. Paul . . .
>
> We are come now to our second generall part . . .
>
> To proceed . . .
>
> This is presented more fully in the text . . .
>
> (II.17.341–5)

Donne is also careful to use his basic text as a motif in the sermon structure, restating it, or part of it, as a way of keeping the audience fixed upon the specific matter in hand.

Donne's basic structural devices are obvious enough and quite traditional.[35] They are clearly designed to give his sermons a marked and logical shape, one which is lucid and readily grasped. They indicate a concern with communication and concentration upon the idea of audience, which we should expect given the medium and the drives of Donne's writing as a whole, but it would be a mistake to see evidence of structural care as suggesting that Donne's sermons are easily followed in their detail. The style of the sermons qualifies the impression given by the structure, so that a reader (or hearer) seems to have two choices – to rely on sound and repetition for a general impression, or to concentrate hard on precise and at times intricate sense.

No one familiar with Donne's verse will be surprised to find the sermons marked by vividly eloquent phrasing. So in a sermon for the funeral observances for Sir William Cockayne we have:

Though the soule be *in lecto florida*, in that bed which is alwayes green, in an everlasting spring, in *Abrahams bosome*; And the body but in that green-bed, whose covering is but a yard and a halfe of Turfe, and a Rugge of grasse, and the sheet but a winding sheet, yet they are not divorced . . . (VII.10.257–8)

Nor will such a reader find anything strange in Donne's use of such devices as listing, as at the conclusion of a 1627 Paul's Cross sermon:

. . . if we must pay our Gold, our Blood, our fundamentall points of Religion, for their friendship, A Fortune, a Liberty, a Wife, a Childe, a Father, a Friend, a Master, a Neighbour, a Benefactor, a Kingdome, a Church, a World, is not worth a dramme of this Gold, a drop of this Blood. (VII.17.433)

Such vividness and such rhetorical building obviously convey points clearly and forcefully, but Donne's sermons also make use of the complexity and allusiveness of his poetry. He quotes the Church Fathers and classical texts, draws on etymology ('The Imaginations, *Ipsa figmenta*, as the originall word *Jetzer* imports', II.6.153), plays on Latin meanings ('It must then first be *cordis* and not *carnis*, and it must be *gemitus* not *rugitus* . . .', II.6.154), and the range of vocabulary is enormous. If the fundamental drive of the structures is towards sharp definition, that of the style is towards complexity, intricacy, and this overall tension is also evident at more local levels. If a reader takes almost any paragraph of some length and analyses it, he or she is likely to notice, on the one hand, the prominence of signalling words and phrases and, on the other, the length and complexity of sentences. The drive to be lucid is very marked, but this should not be confounded with simplicity. There is no sign that Donne is trying to thin out his material for popular consumption.

Donne had a wide contemporary reputation as a preacher.[36] The sermons are rhetorically eloquent and could readily appeal to learned audiences, whicle at their best they have an emotive and emotional quality which could affect the learned and the unlearned alike. Even in cold print it is hard not to be shaken by Donne's recreation of Christ's arrest, trial and execution at the end of the sermon usually called 'Death's Duel', and by the emotion with which this is related to the audience:

I dare scarce ask thee whither thou wentest, or how thou disposedst of thy self, when it grew darke & after last night: If that time were spent in a holy recommendation of thy selfe to God, and a submission of thy will to his, It was spent in a conformity to him. (X.11.246)

The ability to be concrete and precise usually keeps the sermons from becoming arid or abstract, while the rhythmical range and variety work to hold the attention, at least in the short and middle terms.

But the manner remains that of the authoritarian. The intricacy and shapeliness are set up against the very idea of the impromptu sermon given by anyone moved by the spirit to utterance. Donne can speak *to* the Common Person, but he makes few concessions and certainly does not speak *for* such a person. Rather, the effect is to dazzle the Common Person with reference and rhetoric and the effort is (validly) to claim kinship with the learned. Speaking to, rather than for, the Common Person, along a line which separates the learned from the unlearned can also be read as Donne using a manner for his sermons which, as much as the attitudes of those sermons, identifies him with the socio-political establishment. Display is an important element in this: the sense of cleverness is as strong as in the Satires or *Songs and Sonets*. Donne remains very much a performer and the performance is élitist.

The sermon has a curious literary standing. Historically speaking, it has a type of half-life in the story of the development of English prose. But this half-life is lived out at the margins of the study of literature in our time, and perhaps only manages so much as a half-life because, in the context of the 'development of English prose', the sermon can be studied in extracts (and usually is). This works for Donne's sermons because many passages are most impressive when met in anthologies of English prose, but who reads, or could bear to read, many of the sermons entire?[37]

The real life of Donne's sermons in the late twentieth century is very limited, and the reasons for this are multiple. They include the decay of established religion in the West and the specific decay of Anglicanism, now little more in England than an etiolate memory of an idealised past and a sentimental indulgence for patriots. Another obvious factor is the development of English prose, which has been away from the mannered style of the

sixteenth and early seventeenth centuries. But yet another aspect
of the dying of Donne's sermons in our culture is of particular
interest.

It was suggested earlier that the sermons work hard to voice
the orthodoxies of the early Stuart state church. As such they
perform a function parallel to that of High Anglican sermons of
the Restoration, marked by their advocacy of strong monarchy
and non-resistance. In their own time Donne's sermons could be
seen as important in their articulation of Anglican Calvinism
(modified in Donne's last years by Laudianism) as a *via media*
between Catholicism and extreme protestantism. This importance
is not doctrinal in any autonomous sense. In fact, it arises precisely
because, in this period, religious statements are also socio-political
matters. The Donne who backs first James I and then Charles I
over religious policy is, at the same time, backing their models of
kingship and rule. In that sense Donne's sermons are fully part of
the societies from which they spring, and this gives them an
enduring historical importance.

But it is precisely the position which Donne's sermons adopt in
relation to these societies which has helped to kill them. They
have half-life as patches of brilliant style and because of local
passages marked by intense feeling, but they are effectively dead
less because the nice division and explication of biblical texts has
become a marginal interest than because Donne is endorsing a
tradition which has largely lost its vitality. The voice of the
sermon is seldom heard in our land, but – more important
perhaps – the voice of Donne's sermons is seldom heard even in
our academies because (amazingly for Donne) it is too orthodox,
too much the voice of an historical élite.

Style comes into this. Donne's sermon-prose has a texture
which is simply too dense to have much life now, when the
process of the growth of a more democratic and functional prose
has mercifully driven self-consciously stylish prose to the margins
of attention. But it is more important here to note that the
seventeenth-century prose which is most alive in our culture
(and, of course, all such prose, like all 'literature' is a minority
interest) is that produced by writers struggling to voice the
aspirations of people hitherto largely mute (at least so far as
written expression goes).[38] The study of prose as 'pure style' has
decayed in our academies, and what remains alive is far from
uniform. It includes, for the seventeenth century, the bourgeois

voice of Pepys, the political tracts of Winstanley, the dissenter writings of Bunyan and the remarkable voices of such as Anna Trapnel and the Ranters. This is partly because some of this prose anticipates, in its directness and idiomatic quality, the plain-style of such novelists of the eighteenth century as Defoe and Richardson, but also because it is a democratic voice, one which appeals to a society like ours which has, at least to some extent, a belief in the virtues of democracy. By such an account the minority voices now are those of the great stylists of the tradition of the 'development of English prose'. Except where courses linger devoted to pure study of such development, Clarendon has become the property of the academic historian, Hobbes and Locke that of philosophers and political theorists. Only Milton of the learned prose writers of the century made such prose serve radical thought in a way which keeps his prose genuinely alive late in the twentieth century, and even Milton speaks for the disprivileged in the accents of privilege (which is, of course, a very important example of how a literary tradition can be commandeered on behalf of the 'non-literary'). Donne, however, speaking for the 'haves' in their own tones, fulfils in his sermons what seems to have been the ambition of a lifetime – to be of the élite – and it is this, ironically enough, which has killed his sermons, at least for our time.

V DEPRESSION AND DEATH

There is, however, a coda. Some of the most vital passages in the sermons, passages which continue to have local life, come when Donne is concerned with death and depression, and this allows the suggestion that even the final and most satisfying role, that of preacher-priest in the Anglican communion, did not fully reassure Donne. The 'sin of fear', it can be argued, never finally passes away.

John Carey's best chapter is that on death, which makes it unnecessary to write at length on the subject here. Carey is right, I think, to stress the theatricality of Donne's presentation of death and his consistent attempts to deal with the subject by minimising it. Further, the idea that for Donne 'Death was an insult to his ego' is important.[39] It indicates the strength of that ego but also the challenge of faith. The physical facts of decay are intimidating in their destruction of our bodily reality, and non-believers have to come to terms with this as the end of ego. A Christian, however, must not accept this and has instead to believe in the resurrection, the Last Judgment and an eternity of bliss or torment. Given this belief, the ego survives, for good or ill, but the challenge lies in fully trusting that there is survival of physical decay. The failure of trust is conducive of despair.

Henry Vaughan is convincing when he presents a feeling of the earthly as dross and the mystical impulse of his verse is accompanied by a distaste for the physical which rules out any strong sense of distress over dissolution. George Herbert writes a poetry which is much more anchored in earth but in this poetry the earthly manifestations are guarantees of divine love and can act to destroy anxieties about decay. Such love in Herbert's poetry works to kill Death by establishing finally reassuring continuities between the earthly and the divine.

Donne has little of Vaughan's mysticism and, although he shares Herbert's concern with the earthly, anxiety marks this concern to a degree foreign to Herbert's work. Donne extends analogies in the effort to make the physical prove something about the ineffable and the emphasis is on the search for signs of divine grace rather than upon serene contemplation of the signs as things found and to be trusted. In a poem like 'The Cross', for example, the effect is of the strenuous, witty discovery of crosses in the natural world and of a nagging awareness, by the persona, of what these crosses *should* signify.

We saw earlier that nothingness is one of Donne's fears,[40] and nothingness is cancellation of the ego. Such fear does not seem surprising in the circumstances of the years between marriage and ordination, for in those years Donne was largely a social nothing. But the fear is not one which vanishes with ordination. In 'A Sermon preached to his Maiestie at White-hall, 24 Febr. 1625' Donne contemplates a kind of super-nothing:

> . . . this is a fearefull privation, of the grace of God here, and of the Face of god hereafter; a privation so much worse then nothing, as that they upon whom it falls, would faine be nothing, and cannot. (VII.2.79)

Nothingness and privation are associated with the loss of recognition by God, and as Donne develops the theme it is with a typical emphasis upon self:

> For, as long as God punishes me, hee gives me Phisick ... If God breaks my bones, it is but to set them strayter, And if hee bruse me in a Morter, it is but that I might exhale, and breath up a sweet savour, in his nosethrils ... I had rather God frownd upon mee, then not looke upon mee; and I had rather God pursued mee, then left mee to my selfe. (VII.2.82–3)

Punishment, vividly and physically rendered, means recognition of the ego; 'thinginess' rather than nothingness. But Donne does not find it easy to get beyond such recognition. 'And *if* hee bruse me ... it is *but that*': Donne cannot, it seems, move to the peace of having become 'a sweet savour'.

This sermon advances the claim that although 'God may absent himselfe' it is 'that he may be sought' – 'but hee comes againe, and with the Olive of peace' (VII.2.85), and the sermon ends with the preacher considering a contract:

> ... no bill of Divorce ... No bill of sale, shall stand up to thy prejudice, but thy dejected spirit shall bee raised from thy consternation, to a holy cheerefulnesse, and a peacefull alacritie ... (VII.2.93)

This sums up the tension. A 'holy cheerefulnesse' is a precise and telling phrase which points to something which is realised in many of Herbert's poems, but the 'consternation' and 'dejected spirit' remind us of another type of phrase which runs through the sermon – 'a necessity of perishing', 'Inordinate dejection of spirit, irreligious sadnesse', 'The Wormwood of thy Depression ... The Gall of thy Melancholly', 'this Disconsolate Soule' (VII.2.85, 90–2).

This tension enacts a kind of poise, a pausing between despair and faith, and this is represented in a remarkable passage from a sermon given before the king in April 1627. The text is Mark 4:24 ('Take heed what you heare') and the passage is Donne's conclusion. A sentence of some twenty lines in the standard edition piles up, in an amazingly lucid complexity, a sense of that which enforces despair. The sentence imagines 'the streame of thy Saviours bloud' being turned 'into another channell, and telling thee, here's enough for Jew and Turke, but not a drop for thee', and it then invokes 'that multiplying glasse of Despair' to anatomise Sin, before grasping at the consolation of being seen as saved by being 'washed in the bloud of my Saviour, clothed in the righteousnes of my Saviour, lodged in the bosome of my Saviour, crowned with the merits of my Saviour . . .' (VII.16.413).

What is at stake here, of course, is a soul and its salvation or damnation. The struggle is close to that of the most striking of the religious poems. In Divine Meditations 1 there are the lines:

> Despair behind, and death before doth cast,
> Such terror, and my feeble flesh doth waste
> By sin in it, which it towards hell doth weigh.
>   (ll. 6–8)

In many of these poems this 'weighing' seems to bring the persona close to despair and the effect of the confident imagining of sin and death, when set against the conditional and often hectic effort to envisage a counterweight, is often to suggest that only rhetoric and a fear of the consequences of despair keep catasrophe at bay. In the sermons there is, I think, a change of balance, in that the sharp phraseology of depression and despair is matched by a phraseology of hope which is stronger than is usual in the poems. This change of balance is difficult to assess, however, for it may have as much to do with the imperatives of delivering sermons as with any great increase in Donne's private confidence in salvation.

One of the most famous sermons is 'Deaths Duell, or, A Consolation to the Soule, against the dying Life, and living Death of the Body'. This title is that on the cover of Thomas Harper's printing of what was Donne's last sermon, one which, we are told on the cover, was 'called by his Majesties household The Doctors owne funerall Sermon'. It was delivered at Court on 25 February 1631 and Donne died on 31 March. It seems fitting that Donne's last sermon was given at Court, the focus of his ambitions for so long, and that its subject was death. In it the tension continues, just as the famous story of Donne rehearsing his own final appearance in his death shroud seems to sum up that poise we have been considering.[41] The Droeshout engraving for the frontispiece of 'Deaths Duell' must, according to Bald,[42] have been copied from the drawing of Donne in his shroud which the subject kept at his bedside in his last days. The image seems appropriately ambiguous. As a *memento mori* it confronts Donne with the inevitability of decay, but as an image it recalls bodily life even at the point of life's passing, and Droeshout's engraving lacks any sense of the 'flights of angels' which Horatio summons to sing Hamlet to his rest.[43]

This is not to say that Donne did not die in serene faith and trust. It would be impertinent for an atheist to pronounce on such a matter at such temporal distance; and believers are free to satisfy themselves. But the sermons, as they engage with the inescapability of death, are recognisably the work of a man plagued by a 'sin of fear', even if the public role of preacher–priest finally strenghtened the sometimes tenuous grip on faith.

An Appendix on Criticism of Donne's Writings

I RESPONSES BEFORE THE TWENTIETH CENTURY

The fullest accessible collection of such responses is A. J. Smith's volume *John Donne: The Critical Heritage* (1975). A slighter selection may be found in F. Kermode (ed.) *Discussions of John Donne* (Boston, 1962). The 'Elegies on the Authors Death' printed with Miles Flesher's *Poems by J.D.* (1633) and reprinted by H. Grierson in *Donne's Poetical Works* (1912) provide an interesting illustration of the 'image' of Donne by the time of his death. R. Granqvist's *The Reputation of John Donne 1779–1873* is a useful discussion of the reception of Donne's work in the nineteenth century.

Such items allow a reader to chart movements in Donne's reputation from the seventeenth century to the end of the nineteenth. They also provide insights into what aspects of Donne's work were of most interest and thereby illustrate both features of taste in earlier centuries and some of the ways in which texts are conditional rather than transcendental. Finally, taken together, such items subvert the once-common view that Donne was essentially re-invented by the twentieth century, which is not to deny that Donne in our time is a rather different figure from the Donnes of earlier periods.

II. DISCUSSIONS OF THE EARLY TWENTIETH CENTURY

Some useful material is to be found in Kermode's *Discussions* (above) and in J. Lovelock (ed.) *Donne: Songs and Sonets* (Casebook series, 1973). Two documents are particularly important in the history of Donne criticism: Grierson's introduction to his edition of the poems (above) and T. S. Eliot's essay 'The Metaphysical Poets' (1921). Grierson's introduction and edition (together with his anthology *Metaphysical Lyrics and Poems* (1921) with its introduction) importantly stress the idea of a metaphysical 'school' and

Donne's place at its head. Eliot's essay extends this emphasis, while also linking an interest in Donne with one in French poetry of the nineteenth century. Grierson and Eliot provide the impetus for much of what followed in studies of Donne.

III DONNE IN THE LATER TWENTIETH CENTURY

It is Donne's poetry (and especially the *Songs and Sonnets* and religious poems) which has dominated discussion of his work since Eliot, although Evelyn Simpson published *A Study of the Prose Works* in 1924 (Oxford) and there has been considerable specialised scholarly work on aspects of his prose writing. Some examples of the latter can be seen in A. J. Smith (ed.) *John Donne. Essays in Celebration* (1972).

The concept of a metaphysical school, established by Eliot and Grierson, was developed in the 1930s. G. Williamson, explicit about his debt to Eliot, published *The Donne Tradition* in 1930, while F. R. Leavis in *Revaluation* (1936) briefly and brilliantly extended Eliot's observations in his chapter 'The Line of Wit', importantly stressing Eliot's idea of a 'dissociation of sensibility' in the mid-seventeenth century (an idea which did much to increase interest in metaphysical verse 1600–50, misleading though the idea is). This concern with a school of Donne was taken further by A. Alvarez in *The School of Donne* (1961) and E. Miner in *The Metaphysical Mode from Donne to Cowley* (New Jersey, 1969), both of whom provide a stimulating mixture of scholarship and critical perception.

Over the same period, however, there has been the accumulation of monographs on Donne's poetry, and these have inclined either to handbooks of close reading or to studies which emphasise particular types of context. C. Hunt's *Donne's Poetry* (New Haven, 1954) is sub-titled *Essays in Literary Analysis* and demonstrates well the former inclination, while W. Sanders' *John Donne's Poetry* (Cambridge, 1971) has a wider range but shows a similar preoccupation with detailed discussion of voice and tone. J. B. Leishman's *The Monarch of Wit* (1951) is a more scholarly work, but one of remarkable theoretical and critical naivety. Such works have tended to stress Donne's individuality (here again following Eliot) and to underplay traditions which bear upon his work, but other writers have tried to correct this imbalance. That part of L. Martz, *The Poetry of Meditation* (New Haven, 1954) which is concerned with Donne seeks to place his religious poetry within a tradition of religious meditative theory and practice, while among the monographs D. Guss, in *John Donne, Petrarchist* (1966), is interested in 'Italianate Conceits and Love Theory', and N. Andreasen in *John Donne: Conservative Revolutionary* (New Jersey, 1967) with medieval and sixteenth century Christian love. M. Roston in *The Soul of Wit* (Oxford, 1974) studies Baroque and Mannerist elements in the poetry and W. Zander in *The Poetry of John Donne* (Brighton, 1982) subtitles his study *Literature and Culture in the Elizabethan and Jacobean Period*.

Hunt's book (above) was an extreme example of a New Critical approach, decontextualising individual poems almost completely. Other accounts retain tradition and literary histories, either by looking back from Donne (Guss, Andreasen) or by seeing him as beginning a tradition (Leavis, Alvarez), but there has been a marked tendency to divorce texts from biographical and socio-political considerations and verse from prose. Leishman's handling of biography is elementary; Zander's of the socio-political dimension sketchy. However, John Carey in *John Donne: Life, Mind and Art* (1981) made an ambitious attempt to write of a whole Donne, only to come unstuck through coarseness of response and a failure to understand history adequately. Nevertheless, Carey and Zander have written books which suggest where critical studies of Donne may go in the future. When Smith's collection of *Essays in Celebration* (of the four hundredth anniversary of Donne's birth) was published in 1972 it looked both like a celebration of fifty years of activity in Donne studies and an indication of incipient exhaustion. Since 1972 there have been relatively few books on Donne, but there will be more if serious study of the socio-political context develops, perhaps along the lines suggested by Lauro Martines in *Society and History in English Renaissance Verse* (Oxford, 1985).

Notes

In the notes to each chapter London is, unless otherwise indicated, the place of publication. Dates are of editions used; dates in square brackets are of first publication where this is different from the edition used.

Chapter 1

1. R. C. Bald, *Johne Donne: A Life* (Oxford, 1970).
2. J. Carey, *John Donne: Life, Mind and Art* (1983 [1981]) p. 10.
3. A. Sinfield, *Literature in Protestant England 1560–1660* (New Jersey, 1983).
4. See on this F. Jameson, *The Political Unconscious* (1981).
5. See, for example, P. Laslett, *The World We Have Lost* (1979 [1965]) Chapter IV; and H. Kamen, *European Society 1500–1700* (1984) Chapter I.
6. Bald, p. 27.
7. Although D. Ogg tells us that 'the physicians suddenly leaped into high status by their incorporation into a royal college' in the reign of Henry VIII (*England in the Reign of Charles II* (Oxford, 1984 [1934])) p. 130) it remains true that the profession was widely criticised and not seen as suitable for a gentleman.
8. But see R. Houlbrooke, *The English Family 1450–1700* (1984) Chapter VI, for evidence that this is a more complicated topic than used to be believed.
9. I. Walton, 'Life of Dr. John Donne', in *Lives* (Oxford, 1962 [1927]) p. 23.
10. Walton, p. 24.
11. See B. W. Whitlock, 'Donne's University Years', *English Studies*, vol. 43 (1962) p. 12.
12. Walton, p. 26.
13. Bald, p. 51, but also Whitlock pp. 14–18.
14. The 'Life of Dr. John Donne' seems to have been written not long before its first publication in 1640.
15. Carey, p. 71.
16. See Kamen, Chapter I.
17. The classic sixteenth-century account of social organisation is William Harrison's *Description of England* (1577). See also J. Youings, *Sixteenth-Century England* (Harmondsworth, 1984) Chapter V.
18. For theatrical presentation of this see Thomas Dekker, *The Shoemakers' Holiday* (?1601).
19. For a convenient summary of Cranfield's career see J. Watts in T. Eustace (ed.) *Statesmen and Politicians of the Stuart Age* (1985).
20. Walton, p. 23.
21. Ibid. On the Welsh connection see Bald, pp. 20–2.

22. Walton, p. 23.
23. See A. L. Rowse, *The England of Elizabeth* (1964 [1950]) p. 246*f.*
24. Male primogeniture is the most obvious demonstration of the primacy of the male line. The analogies so often drawn between God as head of everything, king as head of state, and husband as head of family make the same point. Donne treats of the subject in his sermon for Sir Francis Nethersole's marriage. See, G. Potter and E. Simpson (eds) *The Sermons*, Vol. 2 (Berkeley, 1955) p. 17.
25. Perhaps the most vivid example is the network established by Buckingham under James I and Charles I. Sir Walter Scott's novel *Kenilworth* gives a good sense of such careers under Elizabeth.
26. Bacon trailed favourites and holders of major office for years before he broke through into the top levels of administration and power.
27. Youings quotes Sir Thomas Smith as saying, 'Whosoever studieth the lawes of the realm, who studieth in . . . the universities . . . shall be taken for a gentleman.' Youings, p. 321.
28. See P. Finkelpearl, *John Marston of the Middle Temple* (Cambridge, Massachusetts, 1969).
29. R. O'Day points out that tutors' guides for university students sometimes stressed travel as part of a desirable plan of studies: R. O'Day, *Education and Society 1500–1800* (1982) p. 109.
30. This was a problem for Leicester when he led an English army to the Netherlands in 1585 and for Buckingham when he accompanied Prince Charles to Spain in 1623.
31. Lacy, in Dekker's *The Shoemakers' Holiday*, puts love above such service. The king's willingness to forgive such treason indicates his high valuation of love rather than any deprecation of the importance of serving one's country in war.
32. For the quotation and details see Bald, pp. 23–7. None of the John Donnes given in Bald's index seems to be the same as the John Donne of Corpus Christi, Oxford, who, in 1538, was involved in college controversy over the Reformation. This Donne was clearly a supporter of the Old Faith against Reformers: see G. Elton, *Policy and Police* (Cambridge, 1972) pp. 97–9.
33. Bald p. 42.
34. Whitlock, however, says that a good many Catholics did take their degrees, albeit illegally, at least up to 1588: Whitlock, p. 13.
35. See J. Miller, *Popery and Politics in England 1660–1688* (1973) pp. 52–3; and P. McGrath, *Papists and Puritans under Elizabeth I* (1967) especially pp. 100–1.
36. On the insecurity of protestantism early in Elizabeth's reign see P. Williams, *The Tudor Regime* (Oxford, 1979) p. 253*f.*
37. This is, for example, the argument of Robert Southwell's *An Humble Supplication to her Maiestie* [1595] R. Bald (ed.) (Cambridge, 1953).
38. See Southwell, p. 14.
39. Baker, of course, famously speaks of the young Donne as 'not dissolute, but very neat; a great visitor of Ladies, a great frequenter of Playes, a great writer of conceited Verses' (see Bald, p. 72).
40. Bald, p. 43.

41. McGrath, pp. 101–7, 114.
42. See E. LeComte, *Grace to a Witty Sinner* (1965) p. 61.
43. On Mental Reservation see *The Catholic Encyclopaedia*, Vol. X (1911) pp. 195–6.
44. The most elaborate recent attempt to make the dating less problematic is by Helen Gardner in her edition of *The Elegies and the Songs and Sonets* (Oxford, 1965) p. xlviiff. Her argument, however, has not convinced many.
45. Allusions rarely do more than establish that something cannot have been written *before* the thing alluded to happened, while stylistic analysis (by itself) is never conclusive of dating.
46. Finkelpearl, p. 5.
47. There is, however, evidence that Donne gradually became known as a poet outside the Inns. See W. Milgate, 'The Early References to John Donne', *Notes and Queries*, Vol. 195 (1950) pp. 229–31, 246–7, 290–2, 381–3.
48. See, for example, Marston's 'In Lectores prorsus indignos', at the opening of *The Scourge of Villanie*.
49. 'To Sir Henry Wotton', l. 1. (All references to Donne's poems are, unless otherwise indicated, to A. J. Smith (ed.) *John Donne: The Complete English Poems* (Harmondsworth, 1975 [1971]).
50. See A. J. Marotti, 'John Donne and Patronage', in G. Lytle and S. Orgel (eds) *Patronage in the Renaissance* (New Jersey, 1981).
51. H. Peters (ed.) *Paradoxes and Problems* (Oxford, 1980).
52. In *Explorata: or Discoveries*, l. 1201ff, see G. Parfitt (ed.) *Complete Poems* (Harmondsworth, 1975) p. 425f.
53. Peters, p. 4.
54. Ibid., p. 15.
55. Ibid., p. 21.
56. A. Davenport (ed.) *The Poems of John Marston* (Liverpool, 1961) p. 51.
57. Although it seems that Juvenal in fact covered himself by attacking targets from the recent past.
58. For a brief account see H. Smith, *Elizabethan Poetry* (Cambridge, Massachusetts, 1952) p. 249f.
59. There are also a few surviving Latin epigrams, the authorship of some of these being in doubt.
60. Marston, ll. 1–4.
61. Guilpin, *Skialethia*, Shakespeare Association Facsimiles, no. 2 (1931).
62. A. Davenport (ed.) *Poems of Joseph Hall* (Liverpool, 1949) p. 18 (*Virgidimarum* I.vii.7–8).
63. Marston, *Scourge of Villanie*, VII.166–168.
64. Guilpin, 'Satyra Secunda'.
65. Spenser's *Faerie Queene* is the classical example here.
66. Hall, *Virgidimarum*, III.v.1–5.
67. Ibid., III.iii.1–2, 15–16; III.i.81.
68. Marston, 'In Lectores prorsus indignos', ll. 1–3.
69. See Youings, pp. 110–11.
70. Hall, *Virgidimarum*, III.i.70–1.
71. Ibid., IV.i.174.

72. John Webster, *The Duchess of Malfi*, I.i.11–15.
73. See, for example, Juvenal, *Satires*, III.
74. This is the standard view. For some modification of it see C. Haigh (ed.), *The Reign of Elizabeth I* (1984) pp. 21, 55, 69, 141.
75. The standard book on this is J. Peter, *Complaint and Satire in Early English Literature* (1956).
76. Walton's 'Life' stresses this and, although Walton is an hagiographer, there is no reason to doubt his basic truthfulness.
77. See, for example, Haigh, pp. 28–9, 34f, 39.
78. See, for example, the Shorter Oxford English Dictionary definition: 'To utter against (persons or things) words which consign them to evil . . . to anathematize, excommunicate'.
79. See note 44. In what follows 'Woman' is used to indicate 'the idea of Womankind'.
80. George Herbert and Henry Vaughan are examples.
81. Public (boarding) schools seem to breed the same dichotomy.
82. See note 44.
83. See, for example, J. B. Leishman, *The Monarch of Wit* (1951).
84. This remains true, although in a reduced sense, even in the famous account by Roland Barthes of 'The Death of the Author', in *Image–Music–Text*, trans. S. Heath (1977).
85. See Whitlock, p. 7.
86. Along the lines of Leishman's *The Monarch of Wit*.
87. Paradox X.
88. Ibid., ll. 20–3.
89. Problem VII, l. 27.
90. Problem XVIII.
91. See Peter (note 75) and, for the classical tradition, Juvenal above all.
92. The reverse catalogue constitutes a convention in itself, seen, for instance, in Suckling's 'The Deformed Mistress'.
93. I should like to record here my debt to a brilliant undergraduate essay on Donne's presentation of Woman by my former student Sue Lyons.
94. Whitlock, p. 7.
95. Thus the variety of responses which can be found in Spenser's *Amoretti* and *Epithalamion*.

Chapter 2

1. R. C. Bald, *John Donne: A Life* (Oxford, 1970) pp. 109, 128.
2. Bald, p. 129.
3. Bald, p. 130.
4. Bald, p. 128.
5. Bald, p. 129.
6. Bald, pp. 130–1.
7. H. Gardner and T. Healy (eds) *John Donne: Selected Prose* (Oxford, 1967) p. 107.
8. Bald takes a more positive view ('. . . his marriage itself had been a source of sustenance and comfort to him', p. 326) but it seems to

me that he places too much weight on retrospective comments. While it is possible that marriage was some comfort even during the difficult years, the surviving letters suggest that it was frequently a burden.

9. Bald, p. 263*f*.
10. A convenient selection from the surviving letters can be found in *Selected Prose* (note 7 above).
11. *Selected Prose*, p. 119.
12. See Bald's chapter, 'Steps to the Temple'.
13. See, for example, Bald, p. 290*ff*.
14. Bald, p. 286*ff*.
15. See Bald, p. 210*ff*.
16. *Selected Prose*, p. 142 (letter to George Gerrard).
17. I. Walton, 'Life of Dr. John Donne', in *Lives* (Oxford, 1962 [1927]) p. 44.
18. See, for example, R. Mandrou, *From Humanism to Science* (Harmondsworth, 1978) pp. 135–6.
19. Bald, p. 141.
20. Ibid.
21. *Selected Prose*, p. 125.
22. Ibid., p. 141.
23. See Spenser, *Shepherd's Calendar*, 'January' (gloss) and Beaumont and Fletcher, *The Coxcomb*, especially II.i.
24. See R. Houlbrooke, *The English Family 1450–1700* (1984) Chapter V.
25. Ibid.
26. Walton, pp. 27, 60, 40.
27. *Selected Prose*, pp. 123–4.
28. J. Carey, *John Donne: Life, Mind and Art* (1983 [1981]) p. 73.
29. *Selected Prose*, p. 127.
30. *Selected Prose*, p. 134.
31. Bald, p. 326*f*.
32. See, for example, Divine Meditations 4, 5 and 9.
33. *Selected Prose*, p. 126.
34. *Selected Prose*, p. 128.
35. *Selected Prose*, p. 129 (to Goodyer).
36. Rather as, in drama, it would be unwise to discount Hamlet's melancholy simply because melancholy is conventional in the Malcontent.
37. *Selected Prose*, p. 130.
38. Bald, pp. 248–9.
39. An interesting context is provided by C. Haigh, 'The Church of England, the Catholics and the People', in C. Haigh (ed.) *The Reign of Elizabeth I* (1984) p. 195*ff*.
40. *Biathanatos* in *Selected Prose*, p. 26.
41. *Selected Prose*, p. 116.
42. T. Healy (ed.) *Ignatius His Conclave* (Oxford, 1969) pp. 29, 59, 89.
43. On the Bull see P. McGrath, *Papists and Puritans under Elizabeth I* (1967) p. 68*ff*.

44. *Pseudo-Martyr* in *Selected Prose*, p. 49.
45. J. Miller, *Popery and Politics in England, 1660–1688* (1973) pp. 67*ff*.
46. See P. Collinson, *The Religion of Protestants* (Oxford, 1982).
47. See also Chapter 3.
48. *Selected Prose*, p. 136.
49. *Selected Prose*, p. 139.
50. *Selected Prose*, p. 141.
51. *Selected Prose*, p. 147.
52. *Selected Prose*, p. 48.
53. *Selected Prose*, p. 75.
54. See Collinson, *passim*.
55. On the Oath see, for example, McGrath pp. 369–70.
56. Along the lines of the famous formula 'cuius regia cuius religio'.
57. *Selected Prose*, p. 46.
58. *Selected Prose*, pp. 52, 50.
59. Walton, p. 38.
60. Walton, p. 35.
61. Bald, p. 284*ff*.
62. J. B. Leishman, *The Monarch of Wit* (1951).
63. *Devotions* in *Selected Prose*, p. 101.
64. Bald, p. 285*f*.
65. On the definition of gentlemen see K. Wrightson, *English Society 1580–1680* (1982) Chapter 1.
66. *Selected Prose*, p. 59.
67. Healy (ed.) p. xi.
68. Healy (ed.) p. 3.
69. *Selected Prose*, p. 59.
70. *Selected Prose*, p. 152.
71. *Selected Prose*, p. 142.
72. *Selected Prose*, pp. 144–5.
73. *Selected Prose*, p. 145.
74. W. Milgate, 'The Early References to John Donne', *Notes and Queries*, Vol. 195 (1950).
75. On this see J. Caputi, *John Marston Satirist* (New York, 1961) p. 80*ff*.
76. See Chapter 1, note 39.
77. Bald, p. 190*ff*.
78. Bald, p. 195.
79. Walton, p. 35.
80. See W. Trimpi, *Ben Jonson's Poems* (Stanford, 1969 [1962]) p. 60*ff*.
81. Walton, p. 45.
82. Healy (ed.) pp. xxv–xxvi.
83. *Selected Prose*, p. 144–5.
84. Milgate, 'The Early References to John Donne'.
85. Famously by J. Crofts in *Essays and Studies*, xxii (1937).
86. Most famously, 'My mistress' eyes are nothing like the sun' (Sonnet 130).
87. On neo-Platonism and love see R. Wallis, *Neoplatonism* (1972) especially pp. 86–90.

88. See Houlbrooke, Chapter V.
89. See D. Starnes and E. Talbert, *Classical Myth and Legend in Renaissance Dictionaries* (Chapel Hill, 1955) p. 403.
90. See Houlbrook, Chapter V, and Wrightson, Chapter 4.
91. 'An Epistle to a Friend, to Persuade Him to the Wars', l. 49.
92. Spenser's 'Epithalamion' presents a similar view more decorously.
93. Bald, p. 240.
94. In Smith this poem is titled 'An Elegy upon the Death of Mistress Boulstred'.
95. See the medieval poem *Pearl* and the introductory material in E. Gordon's edition (Oxford, 1953).
96. D. Guss, *John Donne, Petrarchist* (Detroit, 1966).
97. See E. Mullin, *The Painted Witch* (1985) *passim.*
98. On the subject of publication see P. Sheavyn, *The Literary Profession in the Elizabethan Age* (Manchester, 1967 [1909]).
99. See Collinson, pp. 31–2 and J. Ward, 'William Laud', in T. Eustace (ed.) *Statesmen and Politicians of the Stuart Age* (1985) p. 61*ff.*
100. See Collinson and Ward, note 99.
101. See, for example, C. Hill, *The World Turned Upside Down* (1975 [1972]) p. 162*ff.*
102. A. Sinfield, *Literature in Protestant England 1560–1660* (New Jersey, 1983) p.10*f.*
103. J. Bossy, *Christianity in the West* (Oxford, 1985).
104. Collinson, *The Religion of Protestants.*
105. See Ward, 'William Laud', p. 68.
106. Although the precise position of a sensitive individual could vary in the period with variation in official doctrinal emphasis, separatism continues to be anathema for most people.
107. See F. Chamberlin, *The Wit and Wisdom of Queen Bess* (1925) p. 59.

Chapter 3

1. I. Walton, 'Life of Dr. John Donne', in *Lives* (Oxford, 1962 [1927]) pp. 45–6.
2. Ibid., pp. 47–8.
3. H. Gardner and T. Healy (eds) *John Donne: Selected Prose* (Oxford, 1967) pp. 145–6. In a sermon of 1627 Donne again emphasises the break: 'I date my life from my Ministery' (G. Potter and E. Simpson (eds) *The Sermons of John Donne*, 10 vols (Berkeley, 1953–62) Vol. VII, 16.403. All quotations from the sermons are from this edition, with reference given within the body of the text).
4. Walton, p. 50.
5. R. C. Bald, *John Donne: A Life* (Oxford, 1970) p. 308.
6. Bald, p. 309*ff.*
7. See P. Laslett, *The World We Have Lost* (1965) p. 97.
8. Bald, p. 326.
9. Ibid.
10. Ibid., p. 427.
11. *Selected Prose*, pp. 148–50.

12. See J. Carey, *John Donne: Life, Mind and Art* (1981) p. 201.
13. Bald, p. 414*f*.
14. Bald, p. 515.
15. *Selected Prose*, p. 170.
16. Walton, p. 49.
17. See 'To Mr. Tilman after he had taken orders'; J. Ward, 'William Laud', in T. Eustace (ed.) *Statesmen and Politicians of the Stuart Age* (1985) p. 78; M. Graves, *The Tudor Parliaments* (1985) p. 90; P. Collinson, *The Religion of Protestants* (Oxford, 1982) p. 96.
18. See Carey, p. 198*ff*.
19. Collinson, p. 96.
20. Tradesmen and women establish themselves, of course, as preachers in the seventeenth century.
21. Bald, p. 434.
22. Bald, p. 433.
23. See p. 96*f*.
24. See C. Belsey, 'Disrupting sexual difference . . .', in J. Drakakis (ed.) *Alternative Shakespeares* (1985) pp. 166*ff*.
25. A famous example of this line of thought is Menenius' fable in *Coriolanus*, I.i.
26. This imagery is exploited by Spenser in his *Shepherds' Calendar*.
27. On this symbolism see J. Goldberg, *James I and the Politics of Literature* (1983).
28. See N. Tyacke, 'Science and Religion in Oxford before the Civil War', in D. Pennington and K. Thomas (eds) *Puritans and Revolutionaries* (Oxford, 1978) p. 73*ff*.
29. Bald, p. 515.
30. Bald, p. 490.
31. Bald, p. 492.
32. Bald, p. 479.
33. Bald, p. 407.
34. See p. 112.
35. See G. Owst, *Literature and Pulpit in Medieval England* (Oxford, 1966).
36. Bald *passim* (see Index, p. 601).
37. As my friend Professor John Lucas remarked to me.
38. On the general topic see J. Harrison, *The Common People* (1984).
39. Carey, p. 230.
40. See p. 48*ff*.
41. Bald, p. 528*f*.
42. Bald, p. 529.
43. *Hamlet*, V.ii.364.

Bibliography

I Primary texts of Donne's works

Gardner, H. (ed.) *The Elegies and the Songs and Sonets* (Oxford, 1965).
Gardner H. and Healy, T. (eds) *John Donne: Selected Prose* (Oxford, 1967).
Healy, T. (ed.) *Ignatius His Conclave* (Oxford, 1969).
Peters, H. (ed.) *Paradoxes and Problems* (Oxford, 1980).
Poems by J.D. (1633).
Potter, G. and Simpson, E. (eds) *The Sermons of John Donne*, 10 vols (Berkeley, 1953–62).
Smith, A. (ed.) *John Donne: The Complete English Poems* (Harmondsworth, 1971).

II Other primary texts

Beaumont, F. and Fletcher, J., *The Coxcomb*.
Dekker, T., *The Shoemakers' Holiday*.
Guilpin, E., *Skialethia*, Shakespeare Association Facsimiles, no. 2 (1931).
Davenport, A. (ed.) *Poems of Joseph Hall* (Liverpool, 1949).
Parfitt, G. (ed.) B. Jonson, *Complete Poems* (Harmondsworth, 1975).
Juvenal, *Satires*.
Davenport, A. (ed.) *Poems of John Marston* (Liverpool, 1961).
E. Gordon (ed.) *Pearl* (Oxford, 1953).
Bald, R. (ed.) R. Southwell, *An Humble Supplication to Her Maiestie*, (Cambridge, 1953).
Spenser, *Poems*.

III Secondary material: Donne

Bald, R., *John Donne: A Life* (Oxford, 1970).
Carey, J., *John Donne: Life, Mind and Art* (1981).
Crofts, J., 'John Donne: A Reconsideration', in H. Gardner (ed.) *John Donne: A Collection of Critical Essays* (New Jersey, 1962).
Guss, D., *John Donne, Petrarchist* (Detroit, 1966).
Le Comte, E., *Grace to a Witty Sinner* (1965).
Leishman, J., *The Monarch of Wit* (1951).
Marotti, A., 'John Donne and Patronage', in Lytle, G. and Orgel, S. (eds) *Patronage in the Renaissance* (New Jersey, 1981).
Milgate, W., 'The Early References to John Donne', *Notes and Queries*, Vol. 195 (1950).
Walton, I., 'The Life of Dr. John Donne', in *Lives* (Oxford, 1927).
Whitlock, B., 'Donne's University Years', *English Studies*, Vol. 43 (1962).

Bibliography

IV Other secondary material used

Barthes, R., 'The Death of the Author', in *Image–Music–Text*, trans. S. Heath (1977).
Belsey, C. 'Disrupting sexual difference . . .', in J. Drakakis (ed.) *Alternative Shakespeares* (1985).
Bossy, J., *Christianity in the West* (Oxford, 1985).
Caputi, J., *John Marston Satirist* (New York, 1961).
The Catholic Encyclopaedia, Vol. X (1911).
Chamberlin, F., *The Wit and Wisdom of Queen Bess* (1925).
Collinson, P., *The Religion of Protestants* (Oxford, 1982).
Eustace, T. (ed.) *Statesmen and Politicians of the Stuart Age* (1985).
Finkelpearl, P., *John Marston of the Middle Temple* (Cambridge, Massachusetts, 1969).
Goldberg, J., *James I and the politics of literature* (New Jersey, 1983).
Graves, M., *The Tudor Parliaments* (1985).
Haigh, C. (ed.) *The Reign of Elizabeth I* (1984).
Hill, C., *The World Turned Upside Down* (1972).
Houlbrooke, R., *The English Family 1450–1700* (1984).
Harrison, J., *The Common People* (1984).
Jameson, F., *The Political Unconscious* (1981).
Kamen, H., *European Society 1500–1700* (1984).
Laslett, P., *The World We Have Lost* (1965).
McGrath, P., *Papists and Puritans under Elizabeth I* (1967).
Mandrou, R., *From Humanism to Science* (Harmondsworth, 1978).
Miller, J., *Popery and Politics in England 1660–1688* (1973).
O'Day, R., *Education and Society 1500–1800* (1982).
Ogg, D., *England in the Reign of Charles II* (Oxford, 1934).
Owst, G., *Literature and Pulpit in Medieval England* (Oxford, 1961).
Pennington, D. and Thomas, K. (eds) *Puritans and Revolutionaries* (Oxford, 1978).
Peter, J., *Complaint and Satire in Early English Literature* (1956).
Rowse, A., *The England of Elizabeth* (1950).
Sheavyn, P., *The Literary Profession in the Elizabethan Age* (Manchester, 1909).
Sinfield, A., *Literature in Protestant England 1560–1660* (New Jersey, 1983).
Smith, H., *Elizabethan Poetry* (Cambridge, Massachusetts, 1952).
Starnes, D. and Talbert, E., *Classical Myth and Legend in Renaissance Dictionaries* (Chapel Hill, 1955).
Trimpi, W., *Ben Jonson's Poems* (Stanford, 1969).
Wallis, R., *Neoplatonism* (1972).
Williams, P., *The Tudor Regime* (Oxford, 1979).
Wrightson, K., *English Society 1580–1680* (1982).
Youings, J., *Sixteenth Century England* (Harmondsworth, 1984).

Index

This index lists the main references to men, women and texts cited in the body of this book. Minor references are not listed.

Bald, R. C., 1, 11, 40, 46, 63, 67, 103–4, 111, 115
Bossy, John, 96
Carey, John, 1, 3, 38, 121
Collinson, Patrick, 96
Donne, John
 (a) life
 (1572–1601), 1–12
 (1601–1615), 40–63
 (1615–32), 101–110
 (b) religious position
 Anglicanism, 96f, 100f, 106f, 110f
 Calvinism, 96f
 Catholicism, 7–12, 26f, 54f, 97, 111
 (c) works
 Anniversaries, 45, 51, 65, 82–4
 Biathanatos, 65
 Elegies (erotic), 33: II, 33; III, 34–5; VII, 35; IX, 37; XII, 37; XVIII, 35–6; XIX, 36
 Elegies (funereal): On Mistress Boulstred, 45, 51; Obsequies to the Lord Harrington, 45; Elegy on the Lady Markham, 52, 83
 Epigrams, 19
 Epithalamia, 79f: Epithalamion made at Lincoln's Inn, 46, 80, 82; An Epithalamion . . . on the Lady Elizabeth and Count Palatine . . . , 47, 80–1; Epithalamion (Somerset/Essex marriage), 43–6, 49, 61, 80–1
 Essays in Divinity, 57
 Ignatius His Conclave, 43, 55–9, 64–5, 69
 Letters (prose): To Henry Goodyer, 49–52, 56–7, 66; To George Gerrard, 65, 104
 Letters (verse): To the Countess

of Bedford, 46–7, 51–3, 57, 61, 84; To Lady Carey and Mrs Rich, 51–3; To Henry Goodyer, 48; To Edward Herbert, 53, 58; To Magdalen Herbert, 61; To the Countess of Huntingdon, 45, 53, 86; To the Countess of Salisbury, 51; To Henry Wotton, 48
 Paradoxes, 16–17, 32–3
 Poems by J.D., 73–5
 Problems, 32–3
 Pseudo-Martyr, 43, 55–9, 69
 Religious poems: 'The Cross', 89, 96; Divine Meditations: (1) 124, (4) 90, (5) 90, (13) 95, (14) 89, (18) 59, 89, 97; 'Good Friday, 1613. Riding Westward', 89–90, 94; 'Hymn to God, my God, in my sickness', 90; La Corona (2), 99; 'A Litany', 96, 99; 'To Mr Tilman after he had taken orders', 104
 Satires, 19–30, 33, 58–9
 Sermons, 104ff
 Songs and Sonets, 72f: 'The Canonization', 47, 76; 'Community', 72; 'The Curse', 72, 76; 'The Damp', 90; 'The Dream', 78; 'The Ecstasy', 76; 'The Flea', 77; 'The Indifferent', 73; 'Love's Alchemy', 72, 79; 'Love's Diet', 75; 'The Message', 74; 'A Nocturnal . . .', 48, 74; 'Song' ('Go, and catch . . .'), 77; 'Song' ('Sweetest Love . . .'), 78; 'The Sun Rising', 77; 'A Valediction: of Weeping', 77

Egerton, Sir Thomas, 3, 5, 6, 11, 40–2, 46–7
Guilpin, Everard, 13, 14, 19, 20*f*
Guss, Donald, 85
Hall, Joseph, 21*f*
Herbert, George, 88, 95–7
Leishman, J. B., 62
Marlowe, Christopher, 14, 19, 33, 95, 112
Marston, John, 13, 14, 18, 19, 20*f*, 39

Milgate, W., 72
More, Ann, 1, 30–1, 40*f*, 49–50
More, Sir George, 40–1, 46–7
Sidney, Sir Philip (*Astrophel and Stella*), 17, 72–3, 75
Sinfield, Alan, 1, 96
Spenser, Edmund (*Amoretti*), 20, 72–3
Walton, Izaak, 2, 4–5, 7, 49, 60–2, 68, 101–2, 104